OUR
SHELTERED
LIVES

OUR SHELTERED LIVES

Fred Bales

To the McGuires,
    Mike & Jeanelle,
May your home be
sheltered from the storm.

Fred Bales

11-7-13

ABQ Press Trade Paperback Edition 2013

ISBN 978-0-9885395-3-2

Cover and interior design by Lesley Cox,
FEEL Design Associates, Taos, New Mexico

ABQ Press, Albuquerque, New Mexico

To the homeless everywhere

Acknowledgements

All writers are obligated to others beyond the characters in their stories. In my case I extend thanks to those who read my initial draft. Foremost were members of a writing critique group whose honesty and encouragement made my story a better one. Writers in their own right, they are Maggie Parks, Bob Gassaway, Dennis Herrick, and Jim Belshaw. Another writer playing a meaningful part in my book is an old and constant friend from boyhood days, Daly Walker. Dr. Walker has experience in the publishing world, including his widely-reviewed and well-received book, *Surgeon Stories*. His encouragement and suggestions for additions to my story came at a crucial juncture on the path to completing *Our Sheltered Lives*.

To my wife, Janice, I owe the debt of spousal support, including debriefing sessions when I returned home from stints at the Albuquerque Opportunity Center. Also, her career of ministering to others of varying backgrounds served as a model for appreciating those individuals perceived as different.

I also thank Judith Van Gieson, of ABQ Press, who contributed meaningfully to this story, including overseeing its publication.

Above all, I am indebted to the sheltered men whom I have known, particularly those chosen to be the heroes for this tale. I cannot know to what degree, if any, I changed their lives, but rest assured that they changed mine.

Author's Note

I looked their way but then looked away. On city streets the homeless entered, crossed, and left my field of vision, further thoughts of them erased. The eternal other, the "they," were not my concern then. They are now.

I have been drawn close to dozens of homeless men by meeting them, hearing their stories, and becoming a more thoughtful individual as a result.

For more than seven years, I have appeared two days a week at the Albuquerque Opportunity Center. More than a safe haven for the homeless, the Center offers pathways into permanent housing, among other services.

Using "appeared" to describe my volunteer hours presents a strange word choice. But what is the term for what I do? Work is not it. Aside from being unpaid, I look forward to my time with the staff and men, more so than in some settings endured in my professional life. Serve, a possible alternative, smacks of a one-sided transaction—the eternal do-gooder in action. Who is being served in a setting characterized by reciprocity? Which side of the client-provider footlights do I belong on, if not both?

When I went to the Albuquerque Opportunity Center, I was sixty-five and retired, yet preoccupied by a nagging need to be useful. I had a history of volunteering, including the Peace Corps two generations earlier, and I needed to get out of the house. I was a needy fellow, wasn't I? Yes, need may define a piece of the volunteering equation.

Whatever the incentive, I found a home with the homeless, forming ties not unlike those that bind an extended family. In this memoir, I hope that relating my experiences conveys that sentiment.

I did not volunteer at the Albuquerque Opportunity Center to write a book. The reverse occurred as the book came to me. After more than three years of knowing the center's staff and men, I concluded that they—and I—had a story that merited an audience. So I began jotting down notes after my mornings with the homeless, not only reporting selected scenes but also analyzing my reactions to my experiences and forming my thoughts about homelessness.

The characters presented in this book are real, as are the events that I witnessed. The reports of past incidents told to me are faithfully reproduced, to the extent that second-hand stories can be accurately shepherded from one source to another.

Some names have been changed to protect privacy. Center staff members have been collapsed in two cases into a composite character to simplify the storyline, as have two of my volunteer counterparts. And my years spent at the center have been condensed. But the homeless men I have known are presented as single individuals who will abide with me in spirit long past the forgetting of their names and faces.

Chapter ONE

Curtis is riding with me to buy cigarettes, his. I am chauffeuring him in the "Gray Ghost," my pet name for the Albuquerque Opportunity Center's battered gray van. For nearly three years I have driven dozens of men from this homeless shelter for cigarette buys, but Curtis's case is unique because he relies on a continual oxygen flow, about a canister a day, to keep him going.

Curtis sits beside me, inhaling from transparent tubes stuck under his nose, his oxygen tank cart listing awkwardly between us. Before long he will shed that gear to inhale smoke from a "Native" cigarette, bought by the carton at the Pueblo Indian Trade Winds convenience store on Albuquerque's northwest side. I fret about an explosion if Curtis gets careless or an oxygen tank valve gives out. Kibitzers assure me that I have nothing to worry about. I wonder.

Luther, another veteran of the streets, perches on a back bucket seat and dominates the scene. "Things are going to hell in a hand basket, Fred. I'm telling you. Nobody cares nothing about nobody else, know what I mean? Soon as I sell my motor home, I'm outta here. I'm telling you."

I nod, the time-tested way to engage Luther in ill-tempered mode.

Luther's ancient motor home sits on the center's back lot, flat tires, worn-out brakes, chipped paint and all. The vehicle represents more than an eyesore because it complicates arranging independent housing for Luther, a rubbery-faced bear of a man, rangy in frame and sporting size 17 shoes. I know about Luther's shoe size, having been present when he was measured for footwear to accommodate diabetic swelling. The shoes cost more than two thousand dollars. I learned that fact by asking the technician who attended to Luther at University of New Mexico Hospital. Later, I learned that Luther's shoe inserts cost more than one hundred-and-fifty dollars a pair.

"Don't tell Jennifer I said this, but the AOC is all fucked up, totally. There are guys in there that give me the creeps." Luther is referring to a center program manager and my overseer, Jennifer Kelly.

Curtis and Luther occupy two of six respite beds at the Albuquerque Opportunity Center, operated under the aegis of the city's Metropolitan Homelessness Project. Men in the center's general population sleep in a cavernous space where seventy-one beds stand in uniform rows, sentinel-like. Those residents are turned out in the early morning, not to return until late afternoon or early evening.

The respite unit serves men with chronic medical problems, ranging from cancer to mental illness. They are not turned out daily. My chief volunteer duty entails delivering respite residents to medical appointments and social service agencies, although I have interpreted my charge broadly enough to accommodate forays to banks and box stores and cigarette shops and one failed assignation. (The woman in question was not available). I religiously bypass liquor stores, however.

Curtis produces a sheaf of bills as we swing into the drive-through at the Trade Winds on our cigarette run. And when a fuzzy, blaring voice assaults us from a pocked-marked squawk box, Curtis wheezes his order, "Native non-filters, a carton." I strain to hear him and relay the order to the box. We creep forward to the yawning service drawer at the pick-up window. "This joint looks like a bank," Luther observes accurately.

Money is exchanged for cigarettes and Curtis grasps his purchase. "This tobacco here comes from the reservations. Ain't no chemicals in this stuff."

My first reaction is that smoker Curtis's concern about a health issue is crack-up ironic. But I stifle that thought, commenting that I was unaware that the native peoples in the West grew tobacco.

"They don't," Curtis informs me. "No, the Indians grow this tobacco out East. Look here at the motto on the pack." I can't divert my eyes from the road and ask Curtis to read the words.

"Okay, it says here, 'Made by the Original Tobacco Traders.' Says the Mohawks out in New York state make these cigarettes."

I respond that I appreciate the loaded word "original." Luther says nothing, and silence reigns for the two-mile return trip to the center.

Unloading outside the windowless, scuffed metal door to the respite unit goes smoothly. Curtis wheels his oxygen tank, asking me to bring an extra from the van's rear compartment. That should see him through another day, even allowing for his running the tanks full bore.

Lifting the rear hatch on the 1994 Toyota Previa van strains my seventy-year-old biceps. The Ghost's door lifters have failed, and no one can locate replacements. "They don't make them anymore," so I am told. I heave the hatch upward, resting it on my back while swiftly inserting a wooden pole between the vehicle's carpeted floor and raised lid. I wrestle a canister out for Curtis and set it aside before extracting an Orange Crush twelve-pack for Luther.

Luther, meanwhile, has managed to hobble into the respite area while carrying two bags of food from Walmart where he toots around in a motorized cart. Luther is making his way back to the van when he intercepts me and his sodas. Given Luther's intake of the drink, I contemplate buying stock in the company. Inside, I place the cans on a common table where the soft drinks are unlikely to be shared.

Luther and Curtis compensate me with polite thanks for their rides. After reversing the hatch-raising process, I take the van into the back parking lot to pull out the remaining oxygen tanks that Curtis ordered earlier from—and I hauled out of—A+R Medical Supply, a sub-ten-minute ride from the center. That visit preceded the cigarette-buying stop, a sequence that fixed priorities in the correct order.

If my experience is indicative, A+R has captured a profitable market niche for its oxygen business, advertised this way:

FULL RANGE OF RESPIRATORY CARE
All Oxygen Therapy, Gaseous & Liquid ~ CPAP
Sales-Rentals-Repairs ~ Delivery Available
CPAP, BLEVEL AND AUTO UNITS
BACK UP UNITS AVAILABLE AT
DISCOUNT PRICES!
CALL FOR MORE INFORMATION

24-HOUR SERVICE
OPEN SATURDAYS

Booster chairs, wheelchairs, walkers, toilet riser seats, and canes for the disabled also are for sale at A+R, not to mention a "Finger Tip Pulse Oximeter" and a "Micro-Elite Portable Nebulizer," whatever those might be.

Befitting a steady customer, Curtis was greeted by name today at A+R. Strapped for cash, he ordered a paltry five oxygen tanks. Tomorrow, the first of the month, another medical insurance check will come his way and he can reload in full. Meantime, he awaits Medicaid. "I can get all I want then," Curtis commented. "Eyeglasses, all kinds of stuff."

Offloading Curtis's oxygen tanks in the center's cavernous back storeroom, I hear Al's voice behind me. "Hi, Fred." Encountering Al cheers me. Al, a Navajo and Albuquerque Opportunity Center *cum laude* graduate, has secured independent housing and employment. Skilled in manual arts, Al was hired early on as the shelter's maintenance man and custodian. His gray-streaked straight hair hangs just off his shoulders and he wears a baseball cap indoors or out. I cannot remember seeing Al bareheaded. I should talk. I rarely doff my baseball cap inside the center.

Al and I make periodic trips to Home Depot where he buys cleaning supplies and assorted hardware. Al needs my companionship because he lacks a driver's license. Also, his government identification card went missing not long ago at a VFW post watering hole where Al joins other military veterans for social hour, or hours. Anyway, who needs a scrap of plastic to know who you are?

I almost rear-ended a car in the Home Depot parking lot a few weeks back, provoking Al's infectious chuckle and me to question how much longer I should be hauling other people around at my age. I cannot imagine doing this routine ten years from now, or maybe even five.

Chapter TWO

The stairs to the Albuquerque Opportunity Center's second floor offices rise at a sharp angle, sixteen steps without a landing. Would any respectable modern building code allow that? Time was when I bounded up and down stairs. No more. Oh, to be fifty again. Plodding-with-knees-burning best characterizes my climb today as it did the first day I came to the center's offices.

Casting my net about in retirement for a volunteer site, I heard about the center and arranged to meet with the Metropolitan Homelessness Project director, Dennis Plummer. He readily welcomed another volunteer to the fold, but with unconcealed amusement corrected my impression that the Albuquerque Opportunity Center building housed a sheltered workshop. I learned that the center offered programs to boost the homeless back onto their individual feet, complementing the roof-over-the-head function. Securing permanent housing still takes priority, augmented by counseling and links to social services.

Because the center founders took pains to avoid the pejorative "shelter" in the title, I try to avoid the term, often failing. The center's literature proclaims a success rate exceeding 30 percent for the permanent housing goal, an impressive batting average by my reckoning.

Because the center's building sits about one hundred feet back from a four-lane thoroughfare in a faded yellow metal building, I went whizzing by it the day of my appointment four years ago. It's easy to miss. Nondescript describes the place, which once served as a truck garage. The center's main dormitory ceiling tops out at about twenty-five feet and until the last year was uninsulated, just metal ribs in parallel rows supporting the roof. The insulation job dented the budget, but the upgrade was advertised as "paying for itself" over time in lower utility bills. Add in the enhanced nighttime comfort for the seventy-plus men sprawled below and the project was money well spent.

Several months ago, bedbugs infested the main quarters and could be detected retreating up the cement-block dorm walls at first light. Kay, a nighttime volunteer, raised a ruckus about the invasion, setting off an all-out extermination campaign. Kay's emails to Dennis Plummer were colorfully direct.

Dennis,

I used to think that the expression 'Sleep tight and don't let the bedbugs bite' was an old spouse's tale. I don't anymore. Those bugs are real and are right here, live and in living color—as in blood.

Whatever it takes to correct this has to be done pronto. Can't you see the headline now? 'Bedbugs find housing in homeless shelter'?

Let me know what you and the board are going to do.

Kay

So cloth partitions between beds in the dorm were yanked out, mattresses inserted into green plastic covers, wooden bedside tables given the heave-ho to be replaced with plastic ones, and an exterminator contacted and contracted. Good night bedbugs.

By annihilating the bugs, the center matched media hoopla over the critters' unwelcome comeback nationally, transforming its space into more sanitary sleeping quarters than some classy motels and hotels I read about.

***

"Armando needs a ride to UNMH today." After her customary upbeat greeting, staff member Jennifer conveys a standard assignment, this time to University of New Mexico Hospital. Jennifer is thirty-ish, pale-complexioned and a case of a good heart and commitment leading to a concrete job. She parents two boys, one in grade school and one pre-school, but the shoulder -to-shoulder necklace tattoo atop her chest does not quite square with the image of young motherhood. I admit that this comment says more about me and my generation than it does hers.

Armando is recovering from a gunshot wound to the gut. I hear from a cohort that Armando and a relative approached a house where they were not included on the approved guest list, and so were not welcomed with open arms but rather open fire. Whatever the details, the incident left Armando with a bulge protruding from his belly and an obligation to appear regularly in court. He is the respite unit's most veteran resident, prevented from reuniting with his Santa Fe relatives until his seeping wound is controlled by the university hospital staff.

A week ago I was treated to a peek at Armando's belly wound. "Hey, Fred, look at this." Armando sat on the edge of his bed, shirt front pulled open. A flaming red, miniature pyramid of skin protruded from his stomach. I humored Armando, but not myself, by eyeing the red blob for a split second.

"As soon as they can stick this thing back in me, I'll be gone," Armando said with a jaunty air, belying his complaints on other occasions about twice-a-week appointments for cleaning and dressing the wound.

Now he prepares to board the Gray Ghost resting at the respite unit's side door. Armando's short, spiked dark hair is sparse but manages to trace the semblance of a hair line. He is smoking and expertly snuffs out a half-smoked cigarette before stashing it in his shirt pocket.

"What time you leaving today, Fred?"

This is Armando code for inquiring whether I will be available to fetch him at the hospital after his appointment. Otherwise, he will have to rely on a lift from busy center staff, or hop a bus.

"No later than 11:30," I reply. My daily clock time at the facility typically spans nine to eleven or eleven-thirty. During my two volunteer mornings a week, I seldom log as many as five hours total. Awaiting calls for return rides amounts to a chancy proposition as many respite residents prefer negotiating the city on their own until late afternoon. I offer Armando the usual encouragement, telling him to call by eleven if he's ready. It all depends on what other tasks await me.

As I drive back from the hospital, I tune the radio to a country music station and crank up the fan speed on the Ghost's air conditioner. It's mid-July, and the air conditioner struggles to overcome the outside temperature. An off-key accompaniment to the music, the vehicle's fan belt squeaks persistently, leading the amateur mechanic within me to speculate about a defective water pump, although I hope that it's a belt noise tied to running the air. I glance down at the dash and see the glowing icon of an oil lamp, reminding me to ask Jennifer about the most recent oil change. Oil changes can be covered, but more complicated repairs represent potential budget-busters for our cause.

Stopping in the AOC's front lot, I kill the engine and enter mileage into a three-ring binder. The form also contains spaces for the date, destination and my initials. The odometer registers 183,049, a numerical indicator of the Ghost's age. All the same, I salute the unnamed citizen who donated the van a few years—and tens of thousands of miles—ago.

Inside, I seek out Al to ask whether recycled clothes are bagged to be "redonated" to another charity. A steady stream of surplus clothing flows into the shelter, even children's and women's clothes occasionally. Whoever accepts these in-kind donations and hands out forms for tax deductions must not screen the clothing all that rigorously. Regardless, what I and the IRS don't know won't hurt anyone, much.

After sorting, usable clothing hangs on metal racks for men upgrading their wardrobes or switching to seasonal outfits. A few goods are upper end, such as the suede jacket I once coveted. But my shopping has been limited to two beat-up baseball caps. My most recent coup was liberating a Pittsburgh Pirates cap, perspiration-tinged and lopsided, that I bestowed upon Brian, the center's exit planner and fellow baseball fan. Brian thanked me, commenting that he would have the cap fumigated before modeling it.

"No nothing today," Al responds to the cast-off clothing question.

For a time, surplus clothes were stuffed into outsized garbage bags and hauled to Thrift Town, a second-hand store in the vicinity. Then Jennifer determined that we should favor a place serving the needy for free. Why not? So for a little more than a month clothing was donated to the Rescue Mission south of downtown. That ended when our loads overwhelmed the mission's needs. Now we favor St. Martin's, a day shelter, or Goodwill as locations for dropping off the bundles each week. Because the bags have a tendency to tear, I have lobbied for sorters to stick clothes into smaller bags, or smaller loads into the giant bags.

Al does have a run for me today, however. "The aluminum is pretty full," he says.

Spent aluminum soda cans are stored in lockers in the parking lot behind the rear storage area. Like surplus clothing, they, too, fill up oversized, black trash bags. The storage units are under lock and key, a precaution brought about months ago after some of the boys raided the stockpile and sold the cans for pocket money. The aluminum proceeds are ostensibly earmarked for holiday parties.

I toss three brimming sacks onto the van's back seats, a tactic that risks soiling the seats but spares me from raising the balky back hatch. The recycle business is less than a mile away, and I pull inside the gate where looming mounds of car hulks, cannibalized refrigerators, and random metal chunks surround a scale centered in a bare-dirt island. The going rate for aluminum these days is fifty-five cents a pound, spelled out on a hand-lettered, irregular cardboard scrap at the entrance.

Spanish is the language of choice here. A young fellow acknowledges me and accepts one sack from my hand. "*Dos más*," I say, using a fragment of Spanish retained from Peace Corps days in Chile. He nods. He weighs the sacks on the low-slung scale, then produces a slip of paper that I carry across the hardpack driveway to a cement-block building where a letter-sized, jagged opening has been cut within a Plexiglas window. "Cashier" is scribbled atop the opening. Iron bars overlay the entire space.

I stand facing the slit until a hand reaches out. I make my offering to the hand and soon it returns with a few bills and change. I look up to spot a shadowy woman's profile behind the opening. The amount on the yellow receipt is recorded in a written scrawl. I count the money: four dollars and thirty-five cents.

When I deliver the proceeds to Jennifer a few minutes later, she thanks me with an "awesome." From someone else, I would rank this as sarcasm, but from her I accept a well-intentioned compliment. She adds, "Armando called. He's ready to be picked up." Jennifer and I know that the second bit of information is redundant.

Armando awaits at curbside as I wheel the Ghost into the hospital's pickup area. In a designated space beside the driveway, several uniformed staff members and people I suppose to be patients are smoking. As we pull away, Armando asks if he can light up and I consent. He rolls down the window and blows smoke toward the open air.

"Mind if we stop at the convenience store?" This also is Armando code, signifying in this instance that he wishes to buy cigarettes.

I answer that the stop poses no problem. The store sits at a corner where I turn on my way back to the center, and I am in no rush today or most days, a luxury of retirement.

If I seem occupied with smoking, I suspect it stems from my circle of friends and acquaintances, few smokers among them. Those that do smoke puff furtively and sporadically, often auditioning various means to quit. The electronic cigarette seems to be the current weapon of choice. And so I notice the smoking habit when it occurs around me. Perhaps it's a class distinction. In my non-tourist experiences abroad, Chile and the Philippines, I noticed chain-smoking even among those clinging to the lowest economic rungs.

Previously, Armando rarely offered opinions or conversation beyond non-committal single sentences. But now as we drive back to home base, he comments on a fellow respite resident when I ask about day-to-day life at AOC.

"Okay, I guess. But Luther, he seems like he's mad all the time. I stay clear of him. I don't think he likes me."

I answer that Luther is a plain-spoken guy who told me that he was a policeman out in Los Angeles, which might explain his less than sunny outlook on the human race.

Armando has shot his conversational wad for the day, but remembers to offer thanks when I drop him at the respite door. Curtis sits outside in a straight-back chair and acknowledges us with a nod and broad grin. Curtis is puffing away, his faithful sidekick oxygen tank standing guard beside him.

I report to Jennifer after the vehicle log book business is performed and then leave after filling in the volunteer sign-out sheet. The sheets bolster official project reports and grant applications by documenting community involvement. The records are kept by month, and I cannot resist leafing through the stack to see how my service at mid-month measures up. My two days a week and total time land me toward the upper half of whatever gold-star volunteer honor roll may exist. But as the cliché has it, you derive more from these experiences than you put into them. And who's keeping score anyway?

Chapter THREE

"Brian's on my case, he's trying to kick my ass out." Luther is bending my ear as I set the Ghost in motion to satisfy his longing for an Arby's roast beef sandwich. Arby's represents gastronomical heaven for Luther, and on this overcast day I agree to transport him to paradise. No other errands claim my attention, and I figure today would be the logical time to honor Luther's frequent hints and outright invitations, accompanied by graphic descriptions of roast beef stacks drenched in a special sauce. Perhaps he should consider a commercial endorsement for Arby's. I could not do the same.

Luther's reference is to Brian's role as exit planner, counseling residents on outside options before they depart. According to AOC Board policy, residents are limited to 30 nights a year at the center, broken up into any mix of weeks or days. In practice, those with housing or job prospects enjoy indefinite extensions. Like Luther, however, respite residents' stays are open-ended.

Luther continues to air his differences with Brian as the Ghost plows its way through rain-splattered streets. Summer months locally are featured as "the monsoon season," signifying that if all goes well the area might be favored with three inches of rain in two months. Desert-bound, Albuquerque averages less than ten inches a year, and in recent years less than eight. For those with not enough to worry about, our drought can fill in the gaps.

"I don't know what I did to piss Brian off, but he's pissed for sure. He wants me to get rid of the motor home—sell it, and get out."

I attempt to steer Luther's thoughts toward long-range housing plans, but this sets off a "human-beings-as-unredeemable-misanthropes" lecture. "I can't afford a place to park the damn thing. People there just rip you off, anyway. Things aren't like they used to be, Fred. Nobody cares nothing for nobody. Know what I mean? There's people out there on the streets you better keep clear of. I'm tellin' you. You watch yourself, now."

Prolonging his monologue, Luther homes in on the center and his bunkmates there—one in particular. "That Armando is another one to watch out for. He about runs respite like a king. What he says there is law, I'm tellin' you. Nobody crosses him, so I just ignore his ass and steer clear of him. That's the only way to play it. Know what I mean?"

Sort of. Not for the first time, I daydream about being mutated into a fly on the wall, in this instance to determine whether Armando's version of respite life or Luther's matches reality, if respite can be said to reflect reality as known by me and other middle-class types. Most of us left dormitory togetherness with strangers behind when we were young.

At Arby's I cover the tab, although Luther makes a show of promising reimbursement. At a window-side table, I sip decaf coffee while Luther smacks his way through a sandwich and curly fries, washed down with an orange soda. He keeps his shaggy head low toward the table top, and I notice that his gray-rimmed glasses have crept down his nose. Luther verges on tears when he thanks me for his treat. "I never dreamed I would get another Arby's this soon. It sure was good."

Mission accomplished.

After dropping Luther at home base, I stop in the front lot and begin work on the mileage log. When I reach the "Destination" space, I hesitate. "Arby's" might raise some eyebrows, assuming that staff monitors log sheets all that closely. Fudging a bit, yet pleased by my resourcefulness, I jot down, "food run" and disembark.

Given my limited hours at the center, I encounter Brian on a hit-and-miss basis. But this day, of all days, Brian strolls by as I'm signing out. Preserving a confidence, I refer to Luther in roundabout fashion. "I see that Luther's motor home is still out there on the back lot."

Brian sighs. In his early 30s Brian is already a veteran social worker. He was an outstanding Boy Scout who kept negotiating the upward trail. He and others like him merit society's thanks.

"We're trying to get the thing up and running, but I don't see how it could pass a safety inspection." Brian shakes his head. "We'll probably have to get it towed out of here. And he doesn't get enough income to afford a decent trailer park. He nets about four hundred a month from Social Security and most places cost at least eight, or more. Anyway, it's way past time to get him relocated."

I suggest that owing to his police officer background, Luther might move into a trailer park—I correct that mentally to "mobile home park"—and catch on as a security guard. I congratulate myself on imagining this future for Luther.

Rolling his eyes, Brian updates Luther's biography for me. "He told you he was an LA cop?"

I bob my head.

"He's told lots of people that. No way. He was a

security guard in a mall, got talked into a robbery with some lowlifes who took advantage of him, and then did a stretch in San Quentin for being an accessory."

There's no reason to doubt Brian's account of Luther's law enforcement career because Brian, like other staff members, is cleared to access locked personnel files. Otherwise, the records are confidential, as is the fact that the men are housed here. Exceptions are made for probation officers and police following up on the whereabouts of convicted child molesters. Callers inquiring about missing persons are told that staff cannot confirm or deny anyone's presence, although a message will be delivered if the man happens to be in house.

Although hardly shocking, Brian's revelation rotates my take on Luther somewhere in the neighborhood of 45 to 90 degrees.

Brian softens slightly. "Luther's not a bad guy, really, but he needs to lighten up. Anyway, about the best we might do is to find a spot where he can park in someone's backyard for two hundred a month with maybe an extension cord run from the house to his trailer."

A strict interpretation of local zoning laws nags at me as I speculate about what an enforcement officer might have to say about such a Rube Goldberg setup.

***

The next day business takes me to the far North Valley to pick up an auto part for my own gray ghost, a 2002 Ford Explorer. It suffered a hit-and-run outside a branch post office while I was in line to buy stamps. The running light assembly was knocked out, the bumper guard sprung, and paint scraped from the sideswipe. I didn't hear the impact, but a witness came into the post office and reported it, describing my SUV to a T.

Feigning nonchalance, I acknowledged owning the victim, saying, "No problem, I've got good insurance." Yes, and watch the premium zoom up after I put in a claim.

My insurance proved good enough, anyway, because I pocketed the $450 cash from the insurance settlement after the deductible, bolted the bumper cover back, and prepaid fifty dollars for a new light assembly at a parts store. Who was it who once advised me to always go for the cash option? I forget. Incidentally, I am not haunted by the specter of having taken bad advice from others, mainly because I tend to ignore advice from others. No, I've made my own colossal blunders. But now and again an exception to the guideline pays off, literally.

While cruising the North Valley, I visit a mobile home park where a hale-fellow-well-met confirms Brian's estimate, quoting $825 a month for parking a mobile home and hooking up to utilities. A stop at a more decrepit place down the road is so disconcerting—complete with its derelict vehicles, rutted gravel road, and a grizzled resident's vacant stare—that I beat a retreat to the security of one of Albuquerque's bustling four-lane streets, albeit many drivers—commuters in particular—would take exception to yoking security and Albuquerque streets within the same sentence.

Driving home after my volunteer hours, I reflect on the homeless, estimated at three thousand to five thousand on any given night in Albuquerque. That perspective makes the center's seventy-one beds, plus the six in respite, seem pitifully inadequate, akin to spitting into the wind. But whatever the numbers, we harbor many hard-core cases who need to be off the streets and safe, if not totally clean.

The numbers are disheartening, indeed. The local public school system identifies about five thousand students a year as homeless. Not long ago I read that the school corporation dedicated a new permanent site for its federally-funded student homelessness project. It provides food and other necessities. What does this amount to in human terms? Are the kids' parents homeless? Are the older ones shifting for themselves? And how many younger ones reside in shelters? The National Center on Family Homelessness reports that families make up the fastest-growing subpopulation. Specifically, families with children account for more than one-third of the homeless, eighty-four percent headed by a single mother.

Two weeks ago I volunteered to act as a chaperone for a field trip involving my granddaughter and her third-grade classmates. When I reported to the classroom, I looked at the children at their desks and questioned whether any of those innocents were counted among the homeless. Before volunteering at the center, that thought never would have come to mind.

In Albuquerque, one major facility shelters homeless families overnight, and its resources are limited. "Resources" seems to be the buzz word in the social service world, encompassing everything from time to talent to treasure—emphasis on the treasure. The Metropolitan Homelessness project has outlined a long-range plan for a family shelter, but good luck in raising funds for that anytime soon. Not enough resources.

During the Great Depression, the homeless ended up in that circumstance when they left their homes or lost their homes and hit the road, riding the rails, cadging food from back doors across the nation, and checking in and out of shanty towns, the infamous "Hoovervilles." Mirroring my current up-close-and-personal relationship with the homeless set, I picture one of those fellows of yesteryear, popularly referred to as hobos or bums or tramps.

The man appeared at our house during my kindergarten year, the last year of the war. My grandmother was keeping house for us while my mother taught school and my dad sailed the Pacific with the U.S. Navy. A knock had brought me running to the outside kitchen door. I opened it as I often did to greet the "meter reader" or a neighbor, but before me stood a gaunt, raggedy man. Grandmother stood behind me and told the visitor to stay put after he asked for "something to eat." I watched my grandmother sliding leftover chicken pieces between slices of buttered white bread, wrapping the sandwich in waxed paper, and handing it to the stranger who mumbled thanks and loped off toward the back alley.

Nowadays I haven't heard about, let alone seen, counterparts to those homeless fellows of old, seeking handouts at private homes. I suppose they exist, but not on the scale experienced during the Depression or even into the war years that framed my earliest memories. We tend to outsource public assistance these days, depersonalize it. Assorted public and private means help patch the safety net we hear so much about, while we discharge our obligations to needy—but unseen—strangers by writing checks to charity. And at times, like Scrooge inquiring rhetorically about work houses and prisons when asked to assist the destitute, we are tempted to mentally call the roll of relevant government programs funded by our tax dollars.

If our rising tide of national wealth since mid-century has lifted all boats—to borrow Jack Kennedy's analogy—we have achieved a higher norm while segregating those who find themselves down and out, or nearly out. Somehow, the Good Samaritan story applies here, but I am parking at a convenience store where I will buy bread and milk, as requested by my wife before I left home.

Chapter FOUR

Curtis's ship has made port in the form of Medicaid, so we set sail for A+R to exchange twelve spent oxygen tanks.

Once there, a blond woman stationed at the counter looks at Curtis, calls him by name, and undertakes the mandatory paper work. Peering into her computer monitor, she acknowledges that Curtis has attained Medicaid. "That's sure better than the 20 limit a month you used to have, isn't it?"

Curtis nods. "Yep, I can get all I want now."

The thirty-something woman pivots to retrieve the tanks to fill our cart. Make that, the cart that I will guide to the Ghost for loading.

Curtis tracks the young woman's path. "Oh, my. Oh, my. Would you look at the ass on that young lady." He wheezes this observation.

Not wishing to ignore him or, worse, be considered a prude, I mumble something about a "scenic rear-end view" and evacuate the area to avoid further anatomical analyses. I feign interest in the nearest display of A+R wares. A booster toilet seat greets me.

As we round out our business, I contemplate a noneventful trip back to the opportunity center. Not yet, my friend.

"Fred, if you don't mind, stop by the Walgreen's down the street or somewhere so I can pick up some milk." Curtis submits his request nonchalantly. "They give us all kinds of cereal but we didn't have no milk today."

I fire off an internal memorandum that my time is flexible. Why should I begrudge this extra errand, or any others, considering that Curtis and his counterparts are cooped up for days on end, relying on me, other volunteers, or staff to escort them to the outside world? The respite unit's dimensions must present a disturbingly confined environment for men having existed for months or years in the open air and circumstances of relative freedom—and danger.

A red light on Lomas brings us to a halt, and Curtis begins shaking his head. "Look at that poor fool over there." Running true to form, Curtis has his hawkeyes peeled for people and events playing out on the byways.

Curtis is looking toward an empty lot where a hoary, ruddy-faced man is flailing his arms windmill-fashion and moving his mouth, talking to himself—or to God-knows-whom. He grabs a cardboard remnant from the ground and flings it toward a nearby sidewalk. Then he kicks at the air, or perhaps at an imaginary demon, and resumes gesturing.

"I know that guy. He was at AOC," Curtis says.

"His stay must have been short."

"Yes, indeed. They had to kick him out. I think they found him a temporary place at the Diplomat." Curtis's reference is to a modest motel where transients find temporary lodging.

The light changes, and as we ride to Walgreen's I reflect on the mentally ill, who often fall through the gaps in the social service grid. The cardboard-thrower should be housed in a safe and clean place, but in all likelihood will be arrested and jailed, if he doesn't die alone first.

We reach the drugstore where I offer to run in alone to save time. Curtis waves me off, saying that he will do his own shopping. He assigns me to fetch the milk, and after I accomplish that I wait near the front register, shifting a plastic half gallon from hand to hand. After many such transfers, Curtis slips into view. He carries a small box that turns out to be a hair-cutting kit.

"Going to do some barbering?"

"Oh, I'm just thinking about it."

Curtis forks over a hundred-dollar bill to the cash-register clerk. She is unfazed by the denomination, although I am fazed. I intend to ask Jennifer why and how Curtis walks around with that kind of cash. I check my watch, calculating that an uninterrupted trip to the center would allow time for undertaking a book-sorting project. This entry on my to-do list relates to a library upgrade. Another detour crops up, however.

"If you can, I need to stop by St. Martin's to pick up my mail," Curtis announces as we pile into the Gray Ghost. I look over at him and smile, noting his perpetual facial stubble that imitates that of the football player Brett Favre. When do these folks shave? Maybe Curtis's barbering kit contains an attachment that preserves a beard at three or four days' growth.

Curtis has a legitimate reason for another stop. Scores of Albuquerque's homeless maintain mailing addresses at St. Martin's Hospitality Center. The day shelter near downtown also provides breakfast, free telephone calls, showers, clothing, and storage, along with counseling and referrals to social services. A recent budget cut has forced St. Martin's to close on Sundays.

Bystanders milling around block the driveway into St. Martin's, but they scatter to allow me to ease in and drop Curtis. Parking in the congested lot is reserved for staff and St. Martin's volunteers, so I back the Ghost out into Third Street and wheel over to the curb. Curtis has warned me that this stop may take considerable time because a long queue forms for the once daily mail distribution. That information brings to mind personal mail call gatherings long ago at Gnaw Bone Boys Camp in Indiana. I haven't had to answer mail call since.

I sit in the van and observe what I and my peers refer to as "street people" make their way to and from St. Martin's. A haggard looking woman, perhaps in her mid-twenties, pushes a baby-occupied stroller; one old fellow whisks by on crutches; another moves along jerkily, as though robot-controlled. He would do better on crutches.

In less time than anticipated, Curtis shows up, clutching a business-size envelope.

"Don't take off just yet," he says, tearing the envelope open at one end. From the corner of my eye, I spy a government check emerge with its characteristic rainbow coloring.

"This here's my Social Security. They owed me some back pay. I just need to see if they got it right." Curtis studies the check before shutting the passenger side door. "Just go around the corner here to the pawn shop. They might cash this for me."

What's one more stop? I hang a right at the next corner and soon Curtis is rolling down his window and looking at a white-haired man on the sidewalk. "That's J. J.," Curtis informs me. "He used to be at the AOC." Curtis hails a shuffling, stooped man outfitted with a rumpled backpack and baggy jeans. "Hey, J. J."

J. J. lifts his eyes from the pavement, pausing an instant before bringing Curtis into focus. He produces a gap-toothed smile and waves in our direction. Traffic forces us to move on. "Me and J. J. had some times," Curtis says.

I remark that Curtis seems to know lots of people around town.

"I do down here."

We progress to the corner where the "Henry's Pawn Shop" sign looms at Mountain and Fourth. I squeeze into a space straddling a "No Parking" zone opposite "Henry's," and Curtis, oxygen tank in tow, jaywalks across traffic lanes to conduct business.

Traffic and time stream by on Fourth Street, and I wonder what is keeping Curtis. I lock the Ghost and head for the pawn shop. Henry's shop is high-ceilinged and yellow-dim, a bleak contrast to the sun-drenched late summer day outside. Curtis stands at a counter, waiting for a woman in a faded red dress to count his money. Portly, she sits at arm's length from a marred wooden desk. At the main counter a sandy-haired man with gold-rimmed glasses asks me my business. I tell him I am with Curtis. He smiles and suggests that I buy a knife, on sale for five dollars. I reply that I have enough knives at home, thanks.

Curtis's transaction moves along snail-like, allowing me to peruse glass-enclosed shelves filled mostly with Native American artifacts—pottery and jewelry dominate—complemented by Southwestern still-life paintings randomly spaced along the walls. I suspect that Native American people desperate for ready cash pawned these objects. Someone who knew collectibles could score bargains at "Henry's."

"She can't get up," says the slick-haired count-er man, jerking his head toward the desk woman. "You ought to see the skin on her ankles. Thin as paper." Could it be that I am in the presence of Henry himself?

A necklace shaped like a choke collar, gleaming with mother-of-pearl inlaid with silver, attracts my in-terest. I blunder by admiring it aloud. The counter man swings into action. He liberates the jewelry from the case and recites its qualities, among them an assurance that the silver is genuine. "It's marked," he says, pointing to black indentations on the reverse side of the piece.

I cite the two-hundred-dollar price tag, and with-out any break in the conversation the woman pipes up. "That one's been around a while. I'll let you have it for a hundred and fifty."

"I'll think about it. My wife has a birthday com-ing up." True, although it's more than three months off. More intriguing to me than the fluctuating price is the woman's assertive use of first-person. Does she own the place by herself? Is Henry no longer with us? Maybe the counter man is Henry, but he and the missus have hit upon a division of labor. He's the front man and she's the brains. This last scenario tickles my fancy.

At last the presumptive brain delivers a thin stack of bills to the presumptive Henry who systematically stacks the money and begins flipping the contents onto the glass top fronting Curtis, one-hundred-dollar bills first. "One, two, three, four, five, six." The counter man hesitates before concluding, "and twenty, forty and five."

This explains where Curtis acquires C-notes.

"Henry" informs Curtis that $26.98 has been withheld as a service charge. Curtis has been here and done this and accepts the tariff impassively. I cringe.

Curtis pockets the money and we leave. Outside, we discuss the pawn shop check-cashing fee. Curtis shrugs. "Yeah, those folks know how to make a buck, don't they?" Running the numbers mentally, I calculate ten percent of Curtis's check amount, divide by half, and reckon that the withheld amount falls below five percent. Further mental gyrations produce four percent as Mr. and Mrs. Henry's bite out of Curtis's money. Put that way, it doesn't seem quite as usurious—just outrageous.

Curtis answers in the negative when I imprudently ask if he maintains a local bank account. I tell him that in my experience a bank will not cash a check for a random outsider. I've tried it. Curtis agrees when I comment that the well-advertised payday loan businesses also amputate an arm and a leg for check-cashing. I make a standard mental note to ask Jennifer if arrangements might be made at a box store customer service desk to better a four-percent take, especially for a U.S. government check, for crying out loud.

Anxious to resume our return leg, I consult my watch only to hear Curtis ask for a side excursion to the Indian smoke shop at the Four Winds convenience center. Why does this updated itinerary not astound me? Merrily, we barrel along.

Belatedly, we cruise into the smoke shop parking lot after I make a wrong turn that lands us on I-40 West instead of the frontage road's direct route. This detour reinforces my self-image of an explorer who tends to feel his way around Albuquerque. I can arrive at most destinations eventually, but don't ask me for directions. Street names don't come easily. I prefer landmarks.

At the drive-in, the squawk box at the inside lane is covered by an "Out-of-Order" sign, causing me to retreat and pull behind two cars in an adjacent lane. Minutes go by before I tumble to the fact that the cars ahead of us should have advanced. The SUV ahead has tinted windows, and Curtis departs the Ghost to discover that the vehicle is unpopulated. We assume that the drive-through is closed today, but I return the Ghost to the lane featuring the dysfunctional box anyway and roll up to the cashier's window.

Surprise. At the window a laconic clerk asks our order. I contemplate asking for a sign on the squawk box proclaiming "Pull Forward" instead of "Out of Order," but instead request Curtis's standard purchase, a carton of Native non-filters. Curtis hands me $27.50, but the clerk intones "Twenty-eight dollars," into the microphone when I pass along the cash. "They just went up."

Curtis seems taken aback at becoming an inflation casualty, but he digs into his pocket for another dollar bill while I return his two quarters. Performing yet another mental calculation, albeit elementary this time, I reckon that a pack of Native's in a carton costs $2.80, a remarkable price, inflation or no, for an item that fetches five dollars and up elsewhere.

"Yeah, people are crazy if they don't buy cigarettes here," Curtis responds to my financial report. "It's all tax free—no federal, no state, no local, nothin'." Why doesn't Armando frequent the Trade Winds store? Maybe he thinks the trip would inconvenience me.

I tell Curtis that his cigarette-buying echoes that of another rider, Joseph, who several months ago routinely visited St. Martin's to buy cigarettes from an entrepreneur, Ron. Ron made daily forays to the Isleta Pueblo south of town to load up on cigarette cartons, reselling packs to St. Martin's clientele for a profit.

"As a matter of fact, I saw Ron today," Curtis says. "He's still there, but he charges four and a quarter now."

I question aloud why Ron doesn't save time and miles by visiting the in-town smoke shop as we do, but Curtis has no definitive answer except to speculate that Ron either has an "in" at Isleta, or our favorite location will not sell in bulk to him. Maybe such a deal constitutes a federal offense. Anyway, I'm beginning to comprehend that the cigarette-buying process is as much a matter of habit as smoking itself.

As for Joseph, Curtis has news about him, too.

"Joe? Little Joe? I know him from way back. He's in the hospital the last I heard. Somebody jumped him."

"I'm surprised. I always thought of Joseph as one street-wise dude."

Curtis nods. "Yeah, but he couldn't stay away from the booze. That's his downfall."

Now I'm ready to shoot up Twelfth Street to Candelaria and head back home. Throttle down, Mr. Speedy.

"Fred, if you would, make a stop at the Lotaburger at Fourth and Candelaria. I didn't have no breakfast." Helpfully, although obviously, Curtis adds, "It's on the way."

Curtis's eagle eye remains on red alert as we head north on Twelfth. "Uhm, boy, I'd like to get to know her." Whatever Curtis's physical liabilities, a weak libido is not among them.

I swivel to my right to spot a shapely woman, clocking in at half Curtis's age, watering a flower garden. Flowing black hair, black Jeans and a form-fitting white blouse meet my glance. This time, I refrain from commenting about appearances. Let Curtis think what he will about my silence and me.

Blake's has no drive-up at our destination. In the restaurant parking lot, I take Curtis's order: a green-chile hamburger and strawberry shake. He hands me a ten, and I undertake the errand while he opens the Ghost's passenger door to light up.

I retrieve the cooked-to-order burger and the shake, and Curtis thanks me as he cradles the to-go sack and his change, closing the door after exhaling toward the outdoors. But the passenger compartment retains a whiff of cigarette smoke as I start the Ghost, fumbling to turn on the fan and open the outside vent.

Breezing down Candelaria we spot a city work crew hovering over a stretch of torn-up pavement. About a dozen men are present along with two large machines, none of the assemblage in motion. Based on Curtis's comments on past rides, I can predict his reaction.

"Look at those guys. Standing around, leaning on their shovels, doin' nothin'. Must be nice to have that kind of job security." He gives out with an indignant huff.

I would classify Curtis as a dissatisfied taxpayer, but I doubt that he is burdened with any tax payments at any level, beyond sales tax.

We return to the center, fifteen city miles and an hour-and-forty minutes after departing. The mileage pales beside my record-setting forty-one miles in a single morning, although that milestone pertained more to poor route planning on my part than to anything else.

Inside respite, I deliver an extra oxygen tank for Curtis, plus his milk and hair-cutting kit, before wheeling around to the rear door and adding eleven oxygen tanks to Curtis's private reserve in the storage area. It's going on eleven, too late in my view to begin book-sorting. I mention this to Jennifer after regaling her with a travelogue featuring my road-warrior exploits with Curtis. She appreciates my adventure and says that the book project can be put off.

Against all odds, I access a mental note and inquire about check-cashing. Jennifer knows all about Henry's Pawn Shop, and we agree that the payday places are infested with sharks. She mentions that Walmart claims to cash checks for a low flat fee. We make a mutual promise to follow through. I log out, filling in a fresh monthly time sheet because August has given way to September. *Tempus fugit.*

Chapter FIVE

Miracle of miracles. Luther is gone. These tidings greet me on Wednesday, my first weekly volunteer day.

Luther departed over the weekend, motor home in tow, or being towed, Jennifer informs me. "Brian came up with a guy who buys rundown motor homes and spruces them up for resale. Luther got twenty-two-hundred dollars—supposedly."

Who says there is no good news? I ask about Curtis and learn that the staff is working to place him with a nursing home that accepts Medicaid. "We got all the paperwork filled out and everything. I'm calling over there today to set up an appointment for Curtis to take a look."

"Does he need a lift to A and R?"

"No, that's another thing. We put him in touch with Hospice and they're delivering his oxygen now. No more A and R trips." Jennifer smiles.

I smile. "You mean it's some other outfit for the oxygen?"

"Yep. I forget their name."

I send up silent thanks to whichever deity rules over the financial investment universe, grateful that I did not take a stock market flyer in A+R or its parent company. This constitutes fantasy good fortune and investing because after 2008 I play the stock market vicariously. Clearly, though, losing Curtis's business means that A+R's bottom line is destined to plunge.

The word "Hospice" raises a red flag. "Curtis is terminal?"

"Afraid so. He has all kinds of health issues, congestive heart failure for one. I can't imagine that he'll last too long."

This prognosis staggers me. I suppose it shouldn't, given Curtis's previous lifestyle and overall physical shape at age 65. "I just thought that with the unlimited oxygen he might be good for several more years." Also, I regard Curtis's rampaging libido as evidence that he is very much alive.

Jennifer asks whether I had observed Curtis's running his tanks at full bore.

"I figured he did, given the number he plows through."

"He's dependent. I've heard that you can get something almost like an addiction to oxygen just like drugs. He needs that oxygen level to ease a feeling of suffocation, but then the lungs become over-saturated. I guess that's better than what he used to be addicted to—crack."

This is my day for updates. Crack addiction is hardly unknown among the homeless population, or anywhere else around the universe, but I had not heard about a degree of dependency on something as life-sustaining as oxygen. Chalk this information up to my oft-repeated mantra: I learn something new every day at the AOC.

As for rides, Jennifer says that although no one in respite is scheduled, Al needs to visit Home Depot to rent a tile cutter. This pleases me, not just because I like Al's company but also because Home Depot intrigues me in a mystifying way. Something akin to a production titled "Fred in Wonderland."

Jennifer has secured a windfall from Arizona Tile Co., an upscale decorating place off I-25 at Albuquerque's north edge. Her cold call paid off because the business had a surplus of one-foot-square, ceramic floor tiles and was eager to donate the lot, including delivery. Al will install them after picking up the tile cutter. I find Al push-brooming in the main dorm, but he halts work readily for our shopping trip. On our way out, he directs me to the library-computer room's cement floor, the 100-square-feet space to be tiled next to the main dorm.

"See, I had to level up that one side over there," Al says, motioning to a swatch of white gunk running along the outside wall. "They must have had some kind of big doorway over there because the whole floor slopes away." Al's surmise no doubt is correct, because the building housed the truck garage in its previous incarnation.

I bend down to observe Al's handiwork, impressed anew by his know-how. If there's any job Al can't perform, I haven't seen it. Major electric work is an exception because he's not licensed. A volunteer electrician, Leo, donates that skill.

In the front lot, I head for the Ghost but Al suggests taking the nearby wheelchair van to avoid a wrestling match with the Ghost's rear hatch.

The wheelchair van came to the shelter two years back, thanks to a Veterans Affairs grant and price-cutting by a local car dealer. The reported cost approached $50,000. It and its counterpart, a transportation vehicle with bench seats, are Ford Econoline 250s. I dub them collectively "the white whales" or individually as "Moby" and dislike driving the beasts. They're unwieldy, as I discovered a few weeks back when attempting a U-turn in the transport van after taking it for a wash. Let's just say that being honked at for the minor infraction of blocking traffic is not an appropriate reward for performing a good deed.

I point out to Al that the wheelchair Moby is cumbersome thanks to the lift apparatus, adding that the transport Moby has restricted space inside the rear door where a seat blocks access. Besides, its floor sits higher than the mini-van's and we are penciled in for some heavy lifting, at least by my definition.

Al ponders this. "Yeah, you're right. We can do this one," he says walking toward the Gray Ghost.

After we pile in and head toward the street, I comment on a banner fronting the self-storage sheds across the way. It advertises 50 percent-off for the first two months' rent. Hard times must cause some renters to empty their storage spaces and sell off some possessions.

Al chuckles. I ask why.

"Oh, that guy over there. He helped me out when I was living in that field next door."

This day delivers one revelation after another. I understood that Al had been homeless for a spell, but not that he had encamped in the former weed-covered lot west of the self-storage sheds. Before a major plumbing wholesaler cleared the space for a warehouse, I had spotted a summer "camper" or two hanging out there under a lone cottonwood tree.

"You weren't in that field in the winter, were you?"

"Oh, yeah." Another Al chuckle. "It got real cold sometimes, but that guy over there gave me coats and blankets from what people left behind. He did."

"You could have frozen to death."

"It happens. But you know that guy he would check up on me in the morning after the coldest nights. And he'd come up to where I was and he'd say, 'Al, you alive?' And I'd laugh and look out from under all the covers and tell him I was okay. Oh, yeah, he was coming over there all the time. That was before I got some regular work."

I've never met the storage shed proprietor, but he must be slated for induction into the "Homeless Supporter Hall of Fame." Charity often seems to flow from unexpected wellsprings.

At Home Depot we park near the tool rental shop appended to one end of the sprawling building. I visited there before with Al when he rented an oversized drill, but this day he veers right—away from the rental room—rather than taking the expected left when we reach the store's main aisle. I ask about this turn of events.

"Oh, I've got to get some goggles and new work gloves first."

I wait for Al near the checkout lanes, a spectator to the passing parade of professional contractors and home-repair wannabes. They impress me as men and women on missions.

Al returns with his necessities and we walk into the rental room. The clerk looks at me but it is Al who speaks up, ordering the tile-cutter. The employee approaches a ceiling-tall metal shelf, inquiring about the size of our tiles. After Al answers, a heftier model is selected. The clerk hoists the cutter onto a cart and rolls the gear to his counter. He asks me how long we will rent the machine. I defer to Al, while finding it telling that the white man behind the counter still assumes that the white man facing him, and not the "Indian", heads up the project.

Al estimates a two-day rental for the tile-cutter, and I recoil at the cost: $60 a day. Maybe I should add Home Depot to my vicarious investment portfolio.

Al hands the center's Home Depot credit card to me. I relay the plastic to the clerk, but after being swiped twice it fails to register in the scanner. The clerk holds it up to the light, noting that the card is warped. Al reports that this happened when the card became over-heated. I decline to press for specifics.

The Home Depot man enters the appropriate numbers into his machine by hand and asks for identification. Again, he looks at me.

I look at Al and Al looks at me. "You have to do this, Fred. I still don't have my new ID." So now by default I am closing this deal, although normally I would not.

Outside, we hoist the Ghost's rear hatch, resting it upon our shoulders until I position an aluminum pole into place for support. It has replaced a wooden one that cracked. We retreat to load the machine. The cutter features a trough underneath to catch water, and I find myself on the saw—and business—end of the machine, its length barely squeezing sideways atop the van's frayed carpeting. Al removes the pole and I guide the hatch part way down and then release it. A loud thud ensues.

Taking the wheel of the Ghost, I whine about the hatch.

Al sympathizes. "I keep telling them it needs a whole new assembly for those lifters back there. I could fix that, but they tell me it costs too much." I seem to recall that the excuse earlier was that the part no longer was available. Anyway, whether "they" alludes to Jennifer or Dennis or the AOC board is not clear, and I won't trouble myself to find out. Weeks ago I concluded that we will enjoy an operable back hatch when the Ghost is retired, replaced by another van.

I inquire about Al's ID. "Yeah, I need to get on that again. Those people must be dragging their heels on this thing." Despite his attitude toward the state bureaucracy, Al seems mildly peeved at most over the ID issue. I trust that no one cards him at the VFW.

Back at the shelter, Al and I set the cutter on a metal stand situated on the outside porch next to the library space. Al is in the tile-cutting business now.

I seek out Jennifer and find her locking up her office. Her older boy is sick and needs tending to at home. I mention that the Ghost is low on fuel.

"If you have time, could you go and fill it up?

"Sure." I fake enthusiasm. But I guess it's my turn after all the driving I do.

Jennifer pulls out a paper-jacketed credit card from her desk along with a dog-eared instruction sheet. "Get a receipt, if you can. Somebody forgot to do that last time." Not I. I haven't bought tax-free gas since W's administration—and with good reason. The instruction sheet is supposed to assist navigating the gas-buying mine field. As a non-profit, the AOC qualifies to load up on gasoline at designated tax-free locations, a tiresome process that goes miles beyond inserting the appropriate card at the pump. No, we must negotiate a maze to gain that subsidy.

When I signed on to transport respite residents to their various appointments—and some extra-curricular shopping—I had not figured on having to go up against the bureaucratic labyrinths attendant to running a charitable organization. I should have known better than to believe that private businesses alone had to stomach such obstacles.

In fact, the last time the Ghost's gas gauge hit the red zone, I put in five dollars' worth at a convenience store to finesse a trip to the tax-free pumps. I let someone else fight that battle. Yes, I'm a bureaucracy-dodger at heart.

This day I take a deep breath and board the Ghost with card and instructions in hand, struggling to adopt a positive attitude toward my assignment, although I can't help but classify it as an ordeal. Put that way, I suppose that I am engaging in a self-fulfilling prophecy.

The filling station lies less than a mile away, south off Candelaria and almost invisible to any motorist cruising by. It has no central building, only a scanner sitting atop a post, plus ten gas pumps ranging from plain unleaded to super unleaded to diesel. During my last infrequent visit, large trucks had been lurking, and for no logical reason I found their presence intimidating. The guys driving those rigs operate in another dimension than the one where the Ghost and I roam.

No giant trucks clutter the lot when I arrive, just an average-sized stake-bed and a van not much larger than mine. So far so good. I stop opposite the first unleaded pump, shut down the Ghost and consult the checklist for buying gasoline.

Insert card at the central scanning location. Check. Enter the mileage. Check. Enter the pump number. Check. Fill tank. Check. Return to the scanner and insert the card. Check. Enter the number of gallons. Check. Opt for a receipt. Check. Retrieve the receipt. Check. Thank you very much. It all seems so straightforward. What could go wrong?

I approach the scanner with pump number and mileage committed to memory. I insert the card, which I pulled from its protective envelope. Cleverly, I recall a lesson from the dim past that—counter intuitively—the card has to be inserted into the machine horizontally with the magnetic strip facing the outside edge of the slot instead of toward its guts. Why?

The card slides in and is removed. I look at the screen. It asks for a pin number. Pin number? That's not on the checklist, but too late I remember that the pin number is crucial to this exercise. Where is the blasted thing? Right. The number is written on the little paper envelope housing the credit card, which at this very moment is keeping the Ghost company on its front passenger seat.

I traipse back to the vehicle, unlock it, and snatch the paper envelope with the pin number and return to the pump. This go-around, after I complete the pin-number stage, the machine informs me that the card cannot be accepted. I try again with the same result. I have been rejected by a machine.

At this point, a driver who has joined our flock walks up behind me. I step aside to let him try his luck, saying, "I think I must have transposed my pin number."

He produces a grim smile. "Well, if you do it wrong three times, the damn thing will kick you off for a whole day. Good luck."

My newfound guide completes his face time with the machine, and I consult the envelope. The pin number is 1704. Shifting my gaze one number at a time from envelope to key pad, I painstakingly make the entry, and from there on the business goes apace. Perhaps it was because I was holding my breath. Machines are funny that way. It's true.

I heed Jennifer's request and return to the scanner after the fill-up to pull out a receipt, which has to be fumbled for within a tiny compartment protected by a sliding plastic door. Naturally, the white receipt is not visible through the door. Thus at first blush, a neophyte customer assumes that the machine failed to print. I found that out, too, on a previous visit after a knight of the road took pity.

Making my way back to the center, I am reminded about my confrontations with things mechanical and technical. My exotic explanation for these skirmishes pretends that in another life I became enraged at some uncooperative machine and attacked it with enough force to cripple it. What other explanation could account for subsequent generations of machines exacting revenge on me?

Parked at home base, I write in the mileage and compliment myself on remembering to tear out the log sheet and set up a new one. That is standard operating procedure after every fill up. And, yes, I found that out via that most effective teacher in history: experience. So as a retired teacher, I'm still being taught.

Inside, I place the mileage sheet, the card and its sleeve, and—not least—an edited gas-purchase checklist inside Jennifer's mail pigeonhole. I edited the checklist by placing the words "Punch in Pin Number" beside a carrot angled between "Insert Card" and "Enter Mileage." I think about calling Jennifer's attention to my update when I arrive tomorrow, but squelch that idea as soon as it surfaces. No good can result from being petty. But you can bet your boots that a machine would belch out a big, fat reminder message if it were involved.

Chapter SIX

Luther is back. His money is not. I hear this latest installment of the Luther saga upon arriving at the center a week after his departure. Jennifer tells the tale. "Luther got ripped off by some woman and her accomplice. He met up with them in a bar and they got all of his cash." Jennifer shakes her head. "Luther thinks that when somebody's nice to him, they're his friend. They're not. You'd think he'd learn by now."

Yes, you would. Typical of turnover at the AOC, Armando moved out over the weekend, according to Jennifer, and is housed at Santa Fe's shelter, St. Elizabeth's. This arrangement alters Armando's plans, as I understood them. "I thought Armando was going to move in with his family in Santa Fe."

"He was supposed to, but then they didn't take him back. His brother likes to drink, and you can't have liquor in a house where someone on parole is living. His brother didn't want to give up drinking."

I speculate about how often that little probation prohibition goes by the boards, given thin resources for probation programs and problems with catching violators in the first place. Sighing, I ask about rides.

"Curtis needs to go to St. Martin's for his mail." Jennifer says this matter-of-factly, but again something is amiss. I must have been misinformed all the way around. "I thought he'd be leaving for the nursing home by now."

"No, the visit didn't go right. They called me and said he was walking around and talking too much when he was over there."

To my nostrils, a noxious odor wafts from this excuse. "Do you think it's because he's black?"

"I thought about that, too. Could be. Stranger things have happened. Anyway, we're looking into another place for him."

Hesitant to reconnect with Luther but needing to talk with Curtis, I head for the respite unit. A daunting flight of stairs, albeit with a landing, drops from the second-story offices to the six-bed space, and I survey the scene below from the top of the staircase. Curtis looks up. Pretending to steer a car in the air, I signal that I'm free to drive him. Fully dressed and ready, he nods. Luther hunches over a white-topped table, slurping through a bowl of cereal. He squints and smiles my way, asking if he can tag along and visit Walmart.

Sure.

On the way to St. Martin's, Curtis's destination, I gingerly approach Luther about his return engagement at the AOC. "So, you couldn't stay away from us, eh, old buddy?"

This provokes a snarl and the not-unexpected Luther rant. He is not smiling now. "Oh, yeah, this is my favorite place, Fred. Yeah, you know how I feel. If I ever see this goddamned place again, it'll be too soon." He pauses. "I suppose you heard what went down with me."

"Just the general outlines."

"Yeah, well, I don't want to talk about it. Those bastards really took advantage of me, I'm tellin' you."

"Can't the police do something?" My query exhibits a prime example of ill-considered interviewing technique.

The snarl this time is ratcheted upward several decibels. "The cops? You're joking. Those clowns won't do anything." Luther's voice is on the rise. "They know who did it. They know, but they won't do nothin'. This town stinks. Know what I mean?"

Not exactly, but why encourage any more invective?

Next to me, Curtis remains silent and rigid. Jennifer had cautioned that he would be sulking—and with cause. He says nothing as I drop him at the day shelter gate and back the van out onto Third Street and park.

Luther, too, seems to have taken a vow of silence, so I prod him about Armando's departure. I know this is risky, considering their mutually-expressed animosity, yet Luther adopts a nearly-avuncular attitude when he answers.

"Yeah, he's gone. But you know just before he left that silly son of a bitch was talking about going after the guy who shot him. Can you believe that? He was all hot to go back to that house and jump the guy. I told him to stuff that idea."

Armando's foolhardiness impresses me, as it does Luther, as the most counterproductive move a probationer could make.

"Curtis got on him, too," Luther says. "He really told Armando off, told him to smarten up and forget what happened. I don't guess you can forget, but you sure as hell don't have to do something stupid like that. What a dumb fuck."

"You can say that again." I censure myself because I didn't intend for Luther to repeat his earthy assessment of Armando.

Curtis has rejoined us, and I anticipate a visit to Henry's. But his mail brings no checks, prompting us to set out on our return leg. At a stoplight, Curtis motions to a white bus on my left. If it were yellow, I would take it for a school bus. "That there's the transfer bus. The sheriff sends prisoners in that one over to the West Side jail."

Curtis's mood seems to have brightened, verified by his next comment. "I've ridden in that one before." He laughs.

Luther also perks up. "Oh, yeah. I know all about that place."

Referencing to the West Side jail reminds me of the old county jail, also on the Rio Grande's far side, which serves the homeless in winter. I bring that up, and as often happens Curtis plugs the considerable gaps in my knowledge.

"That's right. They open it up November 15th and close it down on March 15th. It's not the Ritz but it works. I spent a little time over there, too."

I can't feature an abandoned jail transformed into a welcoming home for men off the street, but suppose that Curtis has it right when he says it works. Maybe I should drive over to take a look, on the off chance of meeting up with former AOC acquaintances.

I ask Curtis about his new oxygen service and he frowns. "They're not so reliable. The other day I called in because my stock was getting low, and it took them until the next day to get to me. I nearly ran out. I'm thinking about going back to A and R."

That would result in a trip down memory lane for me, and him.

Staring down at his oxygen tank, Curtis wheezes and expresses some urgency to return to the center.

"See, I'm almost in the red zone now."

Taking a split second, I glance away from the road to verify that the needle on the clock-like gauge rests on the black line separating white and red. I step on the van's accelerator and it responds. Despite its age and appearance, the Ghost boasts a reservoir of pep.

At the respite door, I help Curtis inside and prepare for the Walmart trip with Luther, who has settled into the shotgun seat.

"Well, Luther, what's next on your agenda?"

"Not anything good, I can tell you that." Just when I figure that we will have a wordless trip, he goes on. "Jennifer is telling me that I have to go into the general population tomorrow. Says I'm walking and getting around too good to be in respite."

"I've noticed that."

"Yeah, well maybe I ought to bust a big-ass rock on my ankle so I could limp around again and stay in respite." For the first time today, Luther lets loose a heartfelt laugh.

Luther disembarks at Walmart's food store entrance and I cruise for a parking spot, locating one less than half-way up the lane perpendicular to the entrance. Perhaps the motor vehicle gods are smiling on me, and I think about a possible sub-deity, a lesser god, that presides over parking encounters. If so, that character rules arbitrarily. Ask anybody.

I remember an errand and go inside. I don't bother to look for Luther, knowing that up to half an hour will pass before he wheels up to the checkout counter in his cart. Instead, I survey the "Money Center" niche, grudgingly admiring Walmart for giving a space-age name to the old-fashioned one, bank.

I want to verify that Walmart cashes checks for a low flat fee. I spy an information card advertising "Check cashing the smart way." Inside concentric orange-and-white circles, the rumored amount appears in bold-faced lettering: $3. The card talks about government and payroll checks being accepted. Any check greater than $1,000 carries a $6 charge. Fair enough.

A lone customer is completing a transaction at the service counter, and I figure that I can move in behind her with time left over to meet up with Luther. The counter woman is trying to smile. The customer is fumbling through her purse. Nothing is being accomplished.

Impatient, I interrupt the inactivity by asking what identification the store requires for check-cashing. The Walmart service woman seems put upon by the interruption, but she answers that a driver's license or the equivalent will do. I thank her and retreat. Given that requirement, Al could not cash a check here, and maybe not the driving force behind my visit, Curtis. What sort of ID does he carry, if any? I ought to know.

Luther has wheeled into the checkout line, his basket laden with All-American food—chips, pudding, peanuts, soft drinks and the like. I stand beside him, inventorying his haul. I chide Luther. "What would your friendly neighborhood nutritionist say about your diet, Luther?"

"Screw your friendly neighborhood nutritionist."

Those would be my sentiments, if I were in Luther's position. I would like to think that I might couch them in less salty language—but maybe I wouldn't. In any event, I suppose I would eat what I darn well pleased.

Back at home base, I help Luther deposit his grocery sacks inside, say goodbye, go through the respite door, out into the main dorm, and then into the adjoining library space to check Al's handiwork.

Uniformly-laid, one-foot-square tiles overlay the cement floor. Al had fretted about matching the brown-and-tan streaked tiles, but he seems to have achieved artistic success. I check around the door jambs and observe that the cutouts have been rendered perfectly. Michelangelo could not have done better. The space has been transformed. I seek out Al to compliment him, and I pass by the pantry area to find him in his digs at the storage room's far end. "Al, I'm impressed with the tile work in the library room. It all came out great."

"Yeah, it's pretty good. But I need to get the borders done on the wall, and there's one place there that doesn't seem quite level yet."

Jennifer has remarked that Al is a perfectionist, and I'm seeing that side now. "Where did you learn to cut and lay tile. Did you go to school?" I catch myself, realizing that I have leaped to the stereotypical assumption that Al would have attended a trade school on his Arizona reservation.

"No, no. I used to help a guy build cabins up in the mountains, and we were doing stone fire places and hearths up there. I just picked it up that way."

Al's nonchalance impresses me. The day that I "pick up" a skill akin to cutting and laying tile will be the day that some intergalactic force has paralyzed the competent working men and women on planet earth, and civilization has been reduced to depending upon the manual-arts challenged.

I check the time. It's shy of eleven, a mite early to sign out. I take this opportunity to dig out four off-brand oxygen tanks that share storage space with Curtis's collection. Two weeks ago when I was loading the Ghost for an A+R run with Curtis, I mixed in the off-brand tanks. Curtis straightened me out, reminding me that A+R tanks are crowned with white tape.

Curtis's words come back now. "Those other ones belonged to George and he's long gone. He won't be back." Jennifer has confirmed this, leaving me to raise some petty cash at the recycle lot around the corner on Edith. I toss the canisters onto the floor behind the Ghost's front seat, taking pains to separate one from another. In previous trips with Curtis, the clanging of tanks as we rounded corners was enough to activate a zombie.

At the recycle center gate I unload one tank, and after I show the scales man this sample, he affirms that we can do business. I tote the other three tanks to him. He weighs all four, pencils numbers on his yellow pad, and I walk to the window where the "hand" and I engage in our ritual transaction. The hand grasps the yellow slip and returns with greenbacks and change.

I count the money, amounting to $6.44. What! I had counted on something approaching four or five dollars apiece for the tanks. After all, they are composed of heavy metal, a fact I can attest to after lifting them for Curtis. Also, chrome fittings crown their tops. Chrome must carry extra value. Next time I'll ask ahead about the payout, although that would raise the dicey prospect of conversing with the hand.

Giving the money to Jennifer I apologize for the paltry amount.

She waves her hand. "Not to worry. The main thing was to get the space cleared out. Any money we get is gravy. Thanks for everything."

I wish I could adopt Jennifer's sunny disposition more consistently, even when I encounter pirates on the seas of life.

Chapter SEVEN

Luther and Curtis have left the AOC and me behind. Jennifer informs me about personnel changes whenever I check in for another two-morning workweek. Given the break between my volunteer stints, I saw neither star passenger off, a regrettable—but common—passing that I have come to accept. Men come and go in a blurry procession. But I should have snapped that when Luther migrated from respite to the general population he and I were not destined to meet again.

Over the years, I've forgotten most men's names, their faces registering hazy shapes in my mental photo album. A few are etched in detail. Luther and Curtis, for instance, will reside longer and in greater detail in that pantheon. Whether I have fabricated an emotional wall between the men and me to cleave acquaintance-ship from friendship, or whether a hard-wired casualness defines these relationships, I don't know. Typically, I do not interact with any rider for more than four or five weeks, translated into ten contact days maximum. Also, we are known to one another by first names. Now and again when I ask Jennifer about someone's status she includes a surname. But first names stick, if at all.

Today, Jennifer relates the particulars that Curtis gained admittance to a nursing home while Luther landed at the Santa Fe shelter, St. Elizabeth's. I heehaw upon hearing that. "Oh, my, isn't that the height of irony, he and Armando ending up in the same place. Wonder how they're doing together. Actually, there's no need to wonder."

Jennifer concurs. "Doubt if there's too much togetherness between those two."

St. Elizabeth's provides services similar to the Albuquerque Opportunity Center, but supports fewer than 30 beds. That condition might force some togetherness.

I ask about rides. None is scheduled, leaving me to contemplate how often I will be piloting the Ghost now that Curtis and Luther are AOC alumni.

Jennifer reminds me about the book-sorting project. To clear the library for Al's tiling handiwork, books were stacked chaotically in the adjoining storage area. The food pantry anchors the space next to the library with Al, his desk, and tools at the far end. Sandwiched in between, men's belongings are tagged on shelves next to a clothes-sorting and clothes-rack area. Awaiting their return to the library, two empty bookshelves, each six feet high, stand sentinel-like in the windowless cavern.

My job calls for a rudimentary book-sort, including discarding the superfluous and inappropriate. Some volumes, such as the ubiquitous *Reader's Digest* hardback fiction, will be palmed off on Goodwill or the like. Those deemed suitable will be delivered to the outlet store operated by Barrett House, the women's shelter. I acknowledge beforehand that my arbitrary culling for Barrett House might cause political correctness watchdogs to bring me up on sexism charges.

Before I head downstairs, Jennifer makes a special request. "When you go through the books, look for a hardback by Justice Cardozo."

That name tests every smidgen of my accumulated justice-system knowledge, including a single year at law school. I've heard the man's name and believe that he was appointed to the U.S. Supreme Court before my birth. I believe he was considered a liberal jurist. Otherwise, I'm clueless. "Why him?"

"Well, some guy keeps calling me and bugging me about that book," Jennifer explains. "He wants it big time, but I have a feeling that it's worth some money."

"Sounds suspicious for sure."

"For sure. He came in one day and donated a bunch of old paperbacks. Then he went rummaging through our collection and glommed onto the Cardozo book. He said we owed him a book because he made a big donation. I told him it didn't work that way. But he won't take no for an answer."

I make a bold-letter mental note to rescue the Cardozo volume from the pile downstairs.

Attacking the project raises the eternal question: Where to begin? One stack lurks under the clothes-sorting table and another sprawls on a lower storage shelf across the way, abutting the shelf where Curtis's used-up oxygen tanks stood. Better to free up room under the sorting table first.

I bend down, knees cracking, and begin lifting books by the armful onto a gray-metal table top. My organizational powers dictate the barebones categories of "Fiction," "Non-Fiction," "Religion," "Barrett House," and "Discards." This taxonomy will suffice for the nonce.

The sort proceeds. *Reader's Digest* volumes are dumped into 30-gallon, black plastic bags. They accumulate rapidly. And although my Barrett House selections could be challenged, I have no trouble directing a book on breast-feeding in that direction, feeling confident that our men will have no hands-on use for that one. As for the numerous romance novels, perhaps I reveal a prejudice by culling the majority for Barrett House. Chalk it up to the romantic in me.

Many holdings consist of B-list mystery and action-adventure novels. Yet a surprising number, to me, represents top-drawer authors: John Steinbeck, Pearl S. Buck, Amy Tan, Jeff Shaara, James Herriot, and David Halberstam, among them. Occasionally, a title gives me pause, as with "A Confederacy of Dunces." I stare at the thumb-smudged paperback, recalling my faculty time at Xavier University in New Orleans. I doubt that I ever would have read that hilarious award-winner unless a local had recommended it. I think of its author, John Kennedy Toole, and his mother who badgered the literary establishment to publish the book after her son's suicide. The book explored many an endearing idiosyncrasy to be found in the city where I observed—and many a time dealt with—more outsized characters than anywhere I've lived. I imagine a gallery of those eccentrics now, concluding that Albuquerque is tame by comparison, although this may be a time for tranquility in my life. As the poet said, "Come grow old with me. The best is yet to be, the last of life for which the first was made." I hope that old boy knew his onions.

Back at my task, I come across more gems. Two mysteries by Agatha Christie appear and three or four by the ex- Jockey, Dick Francis. Good reads. Halberstam's "October 1964" takes me back to that year's Cardinals-Yankees World Series, a pairing I well remember watching on a grainy black-and-white TV with my graduate school roommate. That series produced a self-deprecating comment by a Cardinal relief pitcher who was roughed up by Yankee batters. Afterward, he told reporters that he threw the opposition his "mattress pitch," explaining that he tossed the ball to the plate and the Yankees "laid on it." Funny what you remember— and what you don't.

A few volumes tend toward the racy side, such as Christine Feehan's "Turbulent Sea," with its front-cover blurb: "It's easy for a woman to be swept away." I consider—but reject—forwarding that one to Barrett House.

Al strolls by. "You got a big job there, Fred. Why don't you get some help?"

"I would, Al, but nobody else could figure out my sorting system." My rationale stretches truth to the snapping point, but it provides a cover to maintain a monopoly over the project. Chalk that up to the control freak in me.

Al's mentioning an alternative chore comes as a relief, promising a cease fire in my book battle. "There's four bags of clothes out there in back that Howard sorted." Al never gives an order and infrequently a request for assistance, except for rides. But his oblique reminders are effective.

Howard, a volunteer counterpart, oversees the clothing operation. About once a week, he sets out rejects in the back lot. Bagfuls of them. If Howard can sort donated clothes week after week, the least I can do is sort books one time.

Given its proximity, Thrift Town is my uncommon choice for the clothing drop-off. Again, the heft of the oversized plastic bags troubles me as I wrestle them out of the Ghost and plop them at the second-hand store's loading dock. To date, no staff has been present for intake, only a closed overhead door facing me. Today, however, a grubby-looking fellow parked in a dented and scratched sedan across the way monitors my labors, and as I drive from the lot I leap to the conclusion that he regularly raids the leavings outside the warehouse. He's welcome to what I left.

Soon enough, I'm resuming my library sort, and I congratulate myself on polishing off the pile under the clothes table, placing retained books into plastic crates with sticky-note labels. These will be reshelved. I move across the room to the second staging area. The routine goes on, the lone exception being greater numbers of *Reader's Digest* fiction hardbacks than expected. How many volumes of those exist? Millions? Talk about a dreg on the market, if any market exists for them. Thank heaven and the delegated powers on earth for Goodwill.

Keeping up the pace, I toss aside a couple of soiled, dog-eared paperbacks before the Holy Grail emerges, not unlike those movie scenes when an angelic chorus bellows out a major chord and a blinding light fills the screen. "Cardozo on the Law" reads the title of the navy-blue, leather-bound book in my hands. I note that the jurist's first name was Benjamin. I kid myself by thinking that I knew that all along. The book boasts gilt-edged pages, complete with a silk-ribbon bookmark. I open it and read that the volume comprises a special publication for the American Bar Association. I cradle it as though I were carrying a time bomb and stride upstairs in triumph.

Jennifer is impressed with the find, and we enlist Brian to track down its worth. Brian, a magician on the Internet, soon finds the book listed on Amazon and eBay sites. Several copies are for sale, but after some rough calculations, Brian estimates the book's value between $200 and $300 on the open market.

We howl in unison at this revelation. My snide side emerges, and I lobby for informing Jennifer's persistent caller about our discovery—a catty conversation begun by lauding him for alerting us to the book's value, but then changing course to offer him first refusal rights to buy it at a low-low $250.

Predictably, Jennifer ignores my sarcasm, countering that she will share our find with Dennis, figuring to locate a local buyer for the volume.

Still, I can't resist a parting salvo at the erstwhile donor. "You know, guys, I guess chiselers are chiselers wherever you find them, but I'd like to think that there's a special corner roped off in hell for those who chisel, or try to chisel, social-service agencies. Give me a break."

Jennifer and Brian nod, no doubt picturing me astride my faithful steed, a high horse.

Jennifer moves on to a practical assignment. "Fred, the gray van needs an inspection, and I called around and a station down on Broadway will do it for free. They're having training sessions and we can take the van in tomorrow."

I pick up on the royal "we." "Gee, Jennifer are you going too?"

She parries that bluff. "No, I figure you can handle this all by yourself, Fred. It's just that we're in this together."

"Ah, yes, togetherness. Anyway, I can't imagine that the Ghost will pass, what with its age and that sickly-sweet smell I've been picking up lately from the exhaust."

"Keep your fingers crossed." Heeding her own advice, Jennifer does just that.

I say adios for the day and, preoccupied with a domestic errand on the way home, forget to fill in my time sheet. No worry. I'll remember to account for both days when I sign out tomorrow, although a betting man or woman might lay odds the other way.

***

Next day I greet Jennifer and Brian, pull the Ghost's ignition key from a jumbled assortment inside a metal wall box, and strike out for the inspection station. They wish me much-needed luck.

Outside the station's back entrance, an overhead garage door blocks my way, and I roll down the van's window to holler for someone to open up. The door lifts and I see no vehicles, just people and equipment are on hand. Evidently the Ghost is a special guest, the sole test-taker this morning.

After I pull forward, a white-coated fellow asks me a few questions, records the mileage, surveys the vehicle's registration document, and orders me to restart the engine and remain in the driver's seat. At this point, eight individuals swarm the car, four technicians with four trainees shadowing them. The van's hood goes up and a hose is stuck up the exhaust pipe. Wires are attached to points under the hood, and two inspectors peek under the vehicle. If I were the Ghost I would complain that my privacy was being invaded.

The tech nearest me asks that I rev the engine, which I do delicately until told to stop. Readings are being recorded on a clipboard by a white coat at a master console to my left, while a trainee hovers over his shoulder. Minutes go by and I begin to fear that some fatal flaw has been detected, as with a terminal hospital patient after getting the once-over by a team of physicians.

"You can shut it off now."

Those words are comforting, although the entire team has assembled at the console to peruse the data. The head tech is talking and motioning toward the screen. Time creeps by. My last inspection experience for my own SUV took about one-fourth of this trial by computer. At last, the spokesman carries papers to me with these words: "It passed. It's old but still running within our tolerances."

What was I saying the other day about the motor vehicle god, or gods? He, she, it, or they just earned hearty, silent gratitude from me. I also thank the crew profusely on behalf of myself and the Albuquerque Opportunity Center and ease out onto Broadway. The Ghost seems unusually responsive.

Like someone clutching a winning lottery ticket, for the second day running I ascend the stairs in triumph back at home base and flaunt the inspection document before Jennifer and Brian.

"Unbelievable," is Brian's assessment.

"Somebody up there likes us," adds Jennifer.

"No doubt my presence in the driver's seat was the key to our success," I say with a wink.

I go downstairs and out the front door to place the inspection paper into the Ghost's glove box. I return to the ground floor office to sign out for yesterday and today, thus beating the aforementioned odds. Showing the document to Jennifer and Brian was worth the extra trip into the building. If I've ever put in a more rewarding week at the center, I can't recall it.

Chapter EIGHT

October has arrived, Albuquerque's optimal weather month for my money. Days remain warm but nights turn cool while hot-air balloons paint rainbow colors on the dawn sky, preludes to the Balloon Fiesta's mass ascensions. The month also brings AOC's barbecue dinner, a fund-raiser that generates more entertainment and networking than money. The "Ditch Dogs," a local band whose members hold day jobs, donate the musical talent. A popular barbecue restaurant cuts its head price on the meal, served up on the center's covered portal and consumed at tables in the open-air garden. It's a dusty affair as tables and chairs—and the band—rest on packed earth.

This year brings another outside-the-box assignment for me. I serve as event co-chair, once again agreeing to volunteer for a task before engaging whatever mental filtering mechanisms are left to me. Publicity has to be arranged—along with renewing contacts with the band and the restaurant—volunteers must be recruited, signs and decorations secured, tables and chairs arranged, soft drinks purchased the day of the event, and on and on. Ticket sales at $20 a head enter into the mix somewhere. Because the fund-raiser occurs after mid-month to avoid conflicting with the Balloon Fiesta and other local wing dings, potential inclement weather raises concerns, either rain or cold—or both. Who said never volunteer for anything? Evidently, I wasn't around at the time or, more likely, not paying attention.

On the evening for the barbecue we are favored with clear skies and 60-degree temperatures. The welcome smell of barbecue floats around the shelter's walled inner courtyard as I arrive, noting that we do not have a sign on the street median out front. We—or precisely I—overlooked that detail.

I appeal to Amanda Clearwater, a can-do staff member who promotes and operates the Community Voice Mail, a project providing private telephone numbers for our men. "No problem," she says.

A two-sided plywood triangle about five-feet tall and spray-painted on both sides for another event sits in the back lot. Amanda leads volunteer buddy Howard and me to the makeshift sign, resembling an oversized sandwich board. She hastens inside, returning with a wrinkled sheet that she effortlessly tears in two. With a staple gun she attaches sheet halves to each side of the sign, my role limited to holding the material in place. Then she produces a spray can and crafts "AOC Barbecue" in bright blue, foot-high letters on each side, complete with arrows pointing toward our event. Voila!

"Now we need a truck to haul this thing out to the street." Amanda says this as Howard and I scramble to be useful. We round up a pickup and together lift our freshly-made sign onto the lowered tailgate and slide it into the bed.

Dodging traffic out front on multi-lane Candelaria Boulevard, Amanda maneuvers the truck in the left turn lane servicing the property as cars and trucks hurtle by. The median narrows at the turning gap, and

I gauge the spot where the sign will not protrude over the cement divider. Amanda backs up to that spot, and Howard and I manhandle the sign off the bed, straighten it and scurry across the street to safety. Amanda toots the truck horn and pulls away.

That task done, I eat barbecue and the trimmings with my wife and two daughters and my grandchildren, listen to the band covering vintage popular songs and, for lack of a better term, mingle. For me, the best aspect of the fund-raiser is meeting people from the center whom I never encounter otherwise, given my limited on-site hours. It's a diverse lot that includes "Spiritual Partners" for men inclined in that direction. No proselytizing allowed.

Middle-aged Ken Jones, our new treasurer, introduces himself, and I am impressed once more with the "happy warrior" attitude displayed by the staff and volunteers. Unlike Howard and me and other retirees, however, Ken works full-time as a bank vice president. Bless him and others like him carving out volunteer time while still in the work force. They are my heroes, causing me to resurrect my line that I volunteer to avoid trouble and boredom in retirement while staying out of my wife's hair. Whatever our varied motivations, however, those of us attached to the Albuquerque Opportunity Center have found a sense of fraternity here.

The band encourages dancing, even on the dirt, but no one responds. No one, that is, except Harold. I knew Harold from driving him to an appointment weeks ago. Now he resides in the general population and for reasons best known to himself is treating us to a one-man show. This stuns me because the Harold I knew was shy, even taciturn. Not tonight.

Harold is stepping out. With a zombie-like stare he gyrates around the ground fronting the band, to their amusement. He flaps his arms, shakes his head, twirls on the balls of his boot-covered feet, and struts across the space as though on stage. I suppose he is in a way. His auburn, stringy hair sails from the back of his head in his self-created windstorm. At one point, a song lyric mentions that the time has come to do something or other, leading Harold to ostentatiously point an index finger at his watch. The crowd of about fifty applauds Harold at the end of the set. He seems spent.

Sitting nearby, Howard expresses my feelings. "He sure surprised me. He never seemed to be all that outgoing when I knew him."

The break brings a scheduled testimony from a former respite rider, Don Barrett. Don is all at once a homeless cliché and a success story. He remembers growing up in Hollywood where his family gained a foothold in the entertainment business. And Don did, too, until he ran afoul of what I label "the deadly parlay": loss of job, loss of spouse, and loss of health. Don personifies that shopworn expression applied to homelessness, "It can happen to anybody." True, many homeless men are cursed with drug or alcohol abuse, or both, but like Don many are not. I have yet to decide whether abusing drugs and alcohol is cause or symptom. I suspect it depends on the individual case.

Upon reflection, I deem "it can happen to anybody" a classic overstatement. I mean, I cannot imagine Bill Gates becoming homeless. But I could imagine it happening to the likes of me, having grown up in a household where the Great Depression was a single memory away, recalled in dreary detail from time to time. I heard then—and I hear now from my men—many a tale involving an unexpected and sheer downward spiral. Each man here has undergone his own Great Depression.

Pale-skinned with gray-streaked hair showing under a flat-billed baseball cap, Don fingers a wireless microphone and introduces himself. He has a job now although not in his old field, producing television videos. He transmits a Buddha-like smile and is steady-voiced as he relates his experience, which he has dubbed "a brush with death." He is comfortable with publicly recounting his time in the homeless wilderness, even writing about it in AOC's newsletter. He plans a book.

"You know my friends, so often we make charitable contributions and never really know the consequences of our actions. I stand before you as living proof that this organization is more than just a way-station from one circumstance to the next, but rather a vital organ of society. Were it to suddenly disappear, the results would be one tragic story after another, not making the headlines, but sculpting the underbelly of the community. Here is my story." Don takes a deep breath.

"After a difficult divorce, I came to Albuquerque to start over in my chosen profession as a writer, producer and director in television and home video. Unfortunately, I discovered that the need for above-the-line creative talent in the industry here wasn't terribly robust. Eventually, I ran out of time, and then I ran out of money.

"One of my brothers, on the street, told me about AOC. How it afforded a safe, comfortable alternative to sleeping on the street, and even had programs to help you jump start your life. I made the necessary call and was offered a bed for 30 days.

"About three weeks into my stay, I became ill one night, so ill that 911 was called and the paramedics were summoned. I didn't know it at the time but I was having a heart attack, and not a minor one.

"I was taken to the hospital and subsequent tests revealed that four of my coronary arteries were blocked. My heart was slowly dying and me with it. The only solution was to undergo open heart, quadruple bypass surgery.

"The state was prepared to cover the enormous costs, but the real problem was recovery. Bypass surgery can take up to a year for a full recovery. I had no place to recover, and without the surgery I had perhaps a month to live.

"Almost at that exact moment, AOC initiated its respite bed program. They convinced the hospital they would give me a secure place to rest and recover, and so the operation was performed. I was on the table for over 12 hours. I still bear the scars where arteries and veins were harvested to replace the blood vessels that were no longer working.

"After ten days in the hospital, I went 'home' to AOC. Everybody was as nice as they could be. They brought me pajamas to wear, books to read, movies to watch. Most importantly they brought me hope. Then, unexpectedly, some of the medication interacted poorly, and within a few days I'd fallen into a coma. Again, 911 was called and I came within about fifteen minutes of dying.

"AOC was so careful that they literally wouldn't let the hospital dismiss me until everyone was certain I was well enough to leave.

"With the help of AOC, Healthcare for the Homeless, and an angel of mercy, a nurse named Mary, I was ready to leave AOC for my own apartment and a job at CompUSA.

"Look at me. I'm an intelligent human being with much to offer society. I would be dead and buried, but these people saved my life. I owe them my very existence. And you, every one of you who contribute to this humane charity, you saved my life as well. Without you there would be no AOC.

"All around us the weather is turning cold. It's just a matter of time before the winter freeze hits. Thousands of men, women and children are on the street, and alas, some of them will die. Now, in these difficult times, we can't save them all. But there's an old saying, tracing to Biblical times, that he who saves one person, it's the same as if he's saved the entire world.

"In conclusion, I thank you and AOC for my life. I also thank you now for the other lives you have saved and will save in the future. You know, at times it's hard to know where your charitable dollar is going. At AOC it is serving the people who need it the most. It is serving those, who for a million reasons, find themselves on the street and against a wall. You are saving lives, and to the best of my knowledge there is no greater human calling. You are special people. You are your brothers' keepers."

Don lowers the microphone and a reverential silence caps his last word, broken by spontaneous applause.

In the afterglow of Don's story, I picture my original encounters with him after his hospital stays. He was quiet and respectful, not at all the image befitting someone who was said to have known such celebrities as Danny Kaye and who had earned big money on the West Coast. He invariably requested, almost apologetically, to be dropped at Fifth and Gold. After a time or two, I tumbled to the fact that he was visiting the main public library.

I approach him at a table after his testimony, praising him on his willingness to stand before a group and relate his experiences and his resurrected life away from the streets. He smiles, saying, "Oh, I remember you."

I remind him that when we first met, I drove him to the library. "As far as I know, Don, you're the only one of my riders to regularly take advantage of that opportunity."

He answers with a self-deprecating shrug. "That place and this one saved my life."

Lead singer Bob Bowman and the band close out the evening with their signature, "Goodnight Louise," a haunting ballad that causes me to conjecture about Irene's fate. Irene must have been jilted.

Pitching in to help with the cleanup later on, PhD Fred Bales and banker Ken Jones stuff trash bags, carry messy serving dishes inside, and perform other menial housekeeping chores alongside AOC staff and residents. And that's as it should be in a fraternity.

Chapter NINE

"I don't know where you're going, Fred, but I'm going with you."

Respite resident Joseph is with us for a return engagement, and his mocking comments accompanied by a series of belly laughs have become something that I anticipate and, for vague reasons, even welcome. As the cliché has it, Joseph and I are on the same page in the book of life, and I am happy to see him back, doubly so after Curtis's report that Joseph had been jumped out on the streets.

Joseph hits his stride when he catches me "feeling" my way around Albuquerque while piloting the Ghost. I continue to bungle my way to most assigned locations, although failing to imitate a crow's flight— or a knowledgeable driver's. Joseph, on the other hand, knows Albuquerque the way I know my backyard. He has lived much of his life not only in the city but also on the city. He is familiar with highways, byways, and bus schedules, and where to find a free meal, and where and when to go for twenty-nine-cent coffee—the Burger King on Carlisle at specified times that he knows by heart. Who needs Rand-McNally or GPS when you have Joseph?

In my latest misadventure, I have managed to turn the wrong way on Mountain Avenue, away from First Street where I intended to drop Joseph for an appointment at Health Care for the Homeless. As we roll east on Mountain, instead of west, I attempt to save a bit of face, if merely a cheek.

"Watch this, my man," I say with false bravado. I execute a hasty U-turn, allowing the steering wheel to fly through my hands as the Ghost completes its 180-degree arc. I feel somewhat vindicated. "What do you think of that?"

But as I complete the turn I am seized by momentary panic, recalling a recent dream where, with Joseph accompanying me, I was hailed by an Albuquerque police officer after a U-turn. Maybe the dream was spawned by guilt from wrongheaded pride over violating traffic laws, or by the thought of Joseph's delighting in my discomfort.

In my dream state, I glanced to my right to see Joseph facing the passenger side's outdoor mirror. "Nice going, Fred, that's really something else all right, except you evidently didn't see that patrol car coming around the corner, the one that's flashing his lights at you now."

No, I didn't— obviously, not evidently.

The officer approached after I pulled the Ghost curbside. He towered above the Ghost, his bulging muscles testing his shirt's outer confines. He appeared to be an affable young man, however. At least he was not frowning. I rolled down the window. He called for license and registration. I obliged with a sheepish smile.

"Sir, did you happen to be aware that U-turns in the middle of a block are illegal in this city, as well as at many designated intersections?" I couldn't discern whether the man in blue was imitating Joseph's sarcasm or plugging in a pat opening.

"Yes, officer, I did know that. But I was in a rush to take my friend here to Healthcare for the Homeless.

He has an appointment and I made a wrong turn."

Joseph was not about to let this opportunity slip by. "Oh, shoot, Fred, you know I wasn't in no hurry to get there. He's just pulling your leg, police man."

I plod on. "Well, maybe he wasn't in a hurry, officer, but I was. I have other riders waiting for me back at the Albuquerque Opportunity Center." I ought to have crossed my fingers when saying that.

Joseph had manipulated me into a white lie, and he was cocked and loaded to run up the score. "Well, now, that's the first I heard of all this, Fred. As a matter of fact, I was there back at the AOC when you asked the other respite guys about rides and nobody said nothing."

This elicited a smile from the officer, who I hoped was sympathetically attuned to our song-and-dance. Also, I may have said the magic words, either Health Care for the Homeless or Albuquerque Opportunity Center, or both. Staff members tell me that the center has a working relationship with the Albuquerque Police Department. Officers have been instructed to take sober, non-violent, and willing vagrants to the center at night rather than haul them off to jail. That saves the police department time and effort. On the other hand, maybe this fellow is amused by seeing Joseph's painting me into a corner.

Whatever the reason, I escaped a fine. The officer was grinning. "Well, sir, I would impress upon you to quit making these turns in the future. And just to make sure of that right now, I'll follow you around the corner to Health Care for the Homeless. It's a good operation."

"Indeed it is," I concurred.

Joseph was relishing his latest triumph. From the corner of my eye, I registered his beaming my way as we rounded the corner onto First. "Lying to an officer of the law, huh, Fred. My, my, what would your mother say about that?"

"Unless you and your big mouth get into the act, she won't know, will she?"

"Maybe. By the way where does your mother live?"

"Indiana."

"Oh, hell, that's too much bother to make a long-distance call. Forget it."

The dream scene fades out, and I snap back into reality, realizing that Joseph is staring at me.

"You all right, Fred. You got awfully quiet there, and you were moving your lips, like in a daze. Don't conk out on me now. If you go down, we're in deep doo-doo because I don't have a driver's license."

I shake my head as though to chase the cobwebs. "I'm with the program now, thanks." I describe my dream.

Joseph replies with a pithy summation. "Yep, Fred, that's about how it would have come down all right."

Joseph has his reward, basking in his imaginary coup and disembarking from the Ghost on the street side opposite Health Care for the Homeless. Customarily, I would execute a time-honored U-turn to drop a passenger directly in front of the pink-adobe building. Today, discretion reinforced by the fantasy patrol car tailing me dictates otherwise.

Joseph fires a parting shot. "See you later, Fred. And take it easy out there, now. I don't know how long you'll last on the streets without me coaching you."

"I'll survive. See you soon. Too soon."

Still chuckling, Joseph slams the door and I pull away, watching as he trudges across the street, his head into the wind on this cool and cloudy November day.

Harking to my teaching days, I aim to treat the homeless men even-handedly, as I tried with thousands of students who passed through my classes. Despite good intentions, some are favored. With students, my prejudices tended toward those showing promise, although a few laggards were prized for their wit. With the homeless, preferences incline toward those who connect with me on equal terms—neither fawning nor aloof—and who eschew self-pity. Joseph passes these tests.

Joseph might have grounds for resentment about his condition. Months ago he underwent a colostomy, but difficulties have arisen in "hooking me back up," as he puts it. He speaks openly—at least to me—about his "crap bag," although I assume that he employs a more scatological term among his cohorts. He has returned to AOC from a second attempt to reconnect the bowel. Weather-beaten and feisty, he is popularly known as "Little Joe." At six-feet-four I am an unreliable judge of others' heights. Most people exist below me. That aside, I would guess that Joseph's altitude falls below five-and-a-half feet. I also would describe him as downright skinny, although his weight is impossible to gauge because of his baggy jeans and loose-fitting shirts, chosen to conceal the "bag." And if anyone needs to know, I pick up a whiff of its contents now and again.

I return the Ghost to the center without any call to execute U-turns, and pull into the front lot. The horizon seems to slant in front of me as I roll to a stop. After logging mileage and all the rest, I hop out to survey the van from the rear. It cants to the right because the rear right tire is flat. Historically, two choices confront me when some mechanical calamity befalls the Ghost: I can consult Al or attempt to cope with the problem by myself.

Making the sensible choice—those familiar with my mechanical disabilities would term it a "no-brainer"—I find Al, who says that if the leak is slow, "we" can pump up the tire until someone finds time to have it patched. I pull the Ghost to the rear storeroom door where Al greets me with an electric-driven air pump, validating my choice twice over.

Rubbing his hands deftly over the deflated tire, Al stops and smiles up at me. "Look here, Fred. There's a big metal piece in here."

I inspect the spot and see a silvery-bright, triangle-shaped metal chunk, not a nail, wedged into the tread. "Wonder what would happen if we pulled that out, Al?" In my imagination, I visualize a scene from a Charlie Chaplin movie or a Laurel and Hardy where a character removes a foreign object from a tire, which spews air akin to a windstorm until our hero reinserts the object with a self-congratulatory nod of the head and rhythmic rubbing of his hands.

"Better not to find out, Fred," Al says, inflating the tire to maximum pressure. "I'll check it tomorrow and hope it's not too flat."

I thank Al and return the van in the front lot.

Upstairs, I run into the crush of a last-minute mailing. The Homelessness project has compiled a list of more than 500 donors and other interested parties who receive newsletters and fund-raising appeals.

"Fred, just the man we want to see." This is Jennifer's standard greeting when I am about to be roped into a task.

I am assigned to peel pre-printed address labels from a slick-backed sheet and stick them onto envelopes housing the latest newsletter. Brian and Dennis and

Amanda are pitching in, too. Is this the modern equivalent of a quilting bee?

Taking up my post, I announce to one and all, "I assume I will be elected to haul these infernal envelopes to the Post Office, what with my successful adventure down there not long ago." Now I'm the one being sarcastic.

Hoots and hollers answer this remembrance of a lowlight experience from my opportunity center past. "Ah, yes, you all obviously recall another chapter in my never-ending, heroic battle with the bureaucracy," I say, flourishing an addressed envelope and stuffing it into a cardboard transport box.

I am referring to the previous mailing of a one-page flyer to announce the fall barbecue. To save resources, the flyer was printed on spare paper of different colors, folded over and stapled to double as an envelope. I should have known something was amiss when everyone else found pressing business when it came time to take the mailing to the Post Office. It hardly bears mention that the unavoidable forms and procedures were put into play, something on the order of magnitude for obtaining tax-free gas. Jennifer assured me that although the Post Office guardians of perpetual nitpicks had dinged us not long ago for daring to submit an outdated form, we were in compliance with the latest regs now.

After taking care of a small, first-class mailing with an engaging employee at the main Post Office, I went around to the bulk mail room where a clerk who turned out to be named Richard greeted me—if you can call it that. I knew I was booked for frustration-city when he intoned with a self-important shake of his head, "You have lots of work to do." That was the harbinger of hassles to come. His first issue was that we did not have the proper permit filled out. Ours was deemed to be out of style, a sin no doubt ranking right up there with wearing white sox with a black funeral suit. No surprise there, I suppose, despite Jennifer's reassurances. Second, he sternly advised that weighing our mailing would present a problem. Why? Because our different-colored papers carried different weights, of course. To the end of my days, I will question whether green weighs more than orange. He then instructed me to place the mailing into cardboard boxes of a certain low-cut type, complaining later that the flyers were overstuffed, requiring transfer to a bigger box.

At one point he left and I was left, too, at the counter to await his return. Before his reappearance, however, a saint of a woman helped me complete the mailing expeditiously, seconds before Richard returned to banter with another clerk while ignoring me. That's when I picked up his first name.

This account conflates about half an hour of torment that prompted me to fire off the following rocket to the postmaster.

Mr. Ronald Kurtz, Postmaster
United States Postal Service
1135 Broadway Boulevard NE
Albuquerque, N.M.

Dear Postmaster Kurtz:

Visiting your main Albuquerque Post Office today I had two positive experiences and one that was far less satisfactory.

My first stop at the main service area was facilitated by the friendly and helpful woman at the philatelic counter who was taking some of the pressure off her co-workers at the counter. She cheerfully took care of business and directed me to the south side of the building and what I have come to refer to as "the bulk mail dark hole."

There I met Richard. Curt and condescending to a volunteer trying to help a charity effect a mailing, he was borderline helpful, with a dash of officiousness tossed in. But the heart of my complaint concerns the time after I had filled out the appropriate forms and returned to his station. He was nowhere to be found. After a wait of almost ten minutes there, a woman who had come on duty at 11 a.m. asked if she could help me, and from then on things went swimmingly.

Now, between my returning to the counter and the cheerful and gracious help from the woman, Richard appeared not once but twice without acknowledging me, or indicating that someone else might assist me, or asking the woman if she were doing so.

I fear that Richard comes up short in the proverbial "people person" department, and as such would be better placed in a position away from encounters with the public. Fine. No doubt plenty of jobs exist where he could be efficiently employed. As is, his manner and lack of attention to this patron renders the name "U.S. Postal Service" an oxymoron.

Sincerely,
Dr. Fred Bales
Professor Emeritus, University of New Mexico

P.S. I would be surprised if this is the first customer complaint about this employee. If so, however, please disregard this letter. All of us are entitled to an occasional off day, even those whose duty it is to serve the public.

Swelled with pride, I hand-carried a copy of the letter around the AOC where the center staff for the most part congratulated me on my pithy prose. Someone, however, I forget who, dubbed it "Fred's rant." Maybe I did overreact, but I had cause.

It seems odd in retrospect that while some popular lore pins pejorative tags on young people—labeling them as too-often impatient, impetuous, and irascible—it is I, the retired professional, who more than once in recent times has demonstrated these traits, rather than the much younger staff. If a recording existed of my ravings at other drivers while piloting the Ghost, I would be vulnerable to blackmail. But I deem it my duty to indulge in such helpful hints to other drivers as, "Get it in gear, Gertrude." Or, "Drive it or park it, Charlie." Maybe someone else besides my latest bureaucrat *bête noire*, Richard, should undergo the oft-prescribed "attitude adjustment." I'll consider it. Meanwhile, I'll check to see whether Albuquerque hosts a Gray Panthers chapter.

Chapter TEN

Joseph is hitching a ride to Burger King on Carlisle by the circuitous way of the downtown Bank of the Southwest. His respite cohort Kelly has bank business and Joseph has lobbied to accompany us for a valid reason: "to get the hell out of here."

I will drop Kelly back at home base—where Joseph could have waited for his ride to a personal rendezvous—before steering the Ghost toward Joseph's destination and then Barrett House, the emergency shelter for single women and women with children. At Barrett House I am scheduled to pick up surplus personal items—soap, shampoo, conditioner, lotion, and the like. It's the holiday season, and the women's shelter is enjoying a donation bonanza.

This bleak, windy day seems determined to prove that December can match January as New Mexico's coldest month. The weather forecast calls for a high in the mid-30s. That's balmy in International Falls, but temperature—like most of my experiences these days—is relative.

Kelly is wheelchair-bound, but with a wedge-shaped torso and Popeye biceps he propels himself hither and yon with little assistance. He wheels the chair to the side of the Gray Ghost, pulls the passenger door open, spins around and hoists himself into the passenger-side front seat. All that remains for me is to fold the chair, giving a tug on its leather seat. Joseph looks on approvingly as I toss the chair into the van. Thanks to my volunteer experience, I have become adept at this routine.

We are en route to town while I fiddle with the heater knobs. This amounts to a useless exercise because the Ghost's heater has conked out, producing a curling mist from the vents when the fan runs.

"Funny, but the air conditioner works fine in summer," I say, trying to stir up conversation. "You'd think that the whole damn thing would go out, both air and heat, at one time."

That sets Joseph off. "Well, Fred, maybe if you'd talk nice to the car it would act better. You really shouldn't swear at something that's taking you some-place. That's my philosophy."

I glimpse daylight and run for it. "I guess this philosophy of yours means that you will be talking nice to me. Right?"

"I said, 'something,' not 'someone.'" I take a glance toward Joseph who looks straight ahead without expression. I accept defeat and ask Kelly about his business, although it's none of mine.

"Just have to make a deposit and get some money back from my Social Security," he answers.

I continue to converse with Kelly, forgoing any more no-win exchanges with Joseph. "How long have you had an account at Bank Southwest?"

"Long time. I can't exactly remember."

We claim a parking place in the bank's back lot. Not wanting to sit in the cold, Joseph and I accompany Kelly into a pristine lobby with its classic marble floors and vaulted ceiling. Kelly rolls up to a desk, rather than to a teller cage, and begins his transaction with the occupant, leaving Joseph and me to stand by at a distance. I look at Joseph and internally criticize his baggy clothes, but then realize that I neglected to shave this morning. Throw in my getup—jeans and a well-worn winter coat, topped off by a sweat-marred baseball cap—and I realize that like Joseph I could pass for a street person.

To break the monotony, I comment on Kelly's bank account. "I don't suppose many guys have bank accounts."

"I sure don't." Joseph's reply is not unexpected, nor the rationale behind it. "I don't trust banks. I keep what I have with me and I'm looking at it right now." Joseph's fixes his eyes on his shoe tops.

I pick up on his meaning, assuming that he imitates a time-honored practice of stashing folding money in one's shoes. "You must have X-ray vision to see all the way through to the bottom of your feet, Joseph."

"Oh, hell, I thought you knew, Fred. I'm Superman." Joseph punctuates his latest witticism with a braying laugh that attracts stares from nearby bank customers and staff.

"Oh, sorry, I forgot," I say, glancing around and praying that we don't become the objects of sustained attention.

Before I can realize what he is up to, Joseph is bolting for a waist-high wooden table holding deposit slips, brochures and—most attractive for Joseph—pens. With a claw-like swoop of his hand that would do an eagle proud, Joseph gloms onto a fistful of ballpoints contained in a black cup, now denuded. "I can use these," Joseph says triumphantly as he stuffs his booty into a patch-pocket of his outer coat.

I look around to confirm my fears and lock eyes with a teller—a twenty-something, well groomed woman—glaring our way.

Having accompanied my riders to many a crowded destination, I have shed layers of social anxiety churned up by the unexpected. And now I rise to an inspired piece of dialogue, if I may say so myself. "It's all right, miss," I assure the teller. "He's a major depositor here." Where did that come from? Wherever, the words amuse the woman who gives out with a tight-lipped smile and busies herself with her cash drawer.

Joseph is delighted. "Way to go, Fred. You're coming along like a champ. I'm beginning to think that with a little more seasoning you might even last a few days on the streets. Now, I think I'll go over and talk with that young lady and see if I can draw out some of that deposit money you're yammering about."

Sober or otherwise, I cannot imagine that conversation.

Kelly rescues us—all right, me—by rolling our way. We exit as I take a parting look over my shoulder toward the teller, tending to whatever business she was engaged in prior to Joseph's raid.

Back at home base, I retrieve Kelly's wheelchair from the back seat and push it to the passenger door. Kelly reaches down from the passenger side of the Gray Ghost to position his chair, and then with one pirouetting motion alights and settles into the seat. I hold the door into respite for him, although he could manage it.

"Thanks, Fred," constitutes his sign off.

Back behind the steering wheel, with Joseph promoted to the front seat, I persuade myself that I have recovered from the U-turn dream debacle on our recent safari to Health Care for the Homeless. I initiate the conversation while we head east on Candelaria toward Carlisle and the Burger King that is Joseph's destination.

"So, Joseph, do they let you have it your way at Burger King?"

"If they let me have it my way, the cops would be over there in a New York minute. But some's better than others at this store. Julie's on today and she don't give me no hassle. I get the discount coffee without a ration of you-know-what. And she lets me hang around as long as I want without buying nothing else."

"You stay in there all day?"

"Oh, hell, no. Just a couple of hours. I'll meet Jimmie there. He's got my sleeping bag and some other stuff that I need to get back."

I resist digging for details about dealings between Jimmie and Joseph. Given Joseph's reputation as an imbiber, I figure that alcohol might figure into the equation.

As we stop at the fast-food place, a fellow who has to be Jimmie looks up and waves, a greeting copied by Joseph.

"Bye, Fred. And by the way, I noticed that you drove over here without getting us lost for a change. Be proud of yourself." He approaches his street companion who carries a sleeping bag that he transfers to Joseph and, talking animatedly, the pair go inside. At least Joseph and Jimmie have a warm place to pass part of this dreary day.

***

Barrett House reeks of security and justifiably so, as I see it. Many women here have escaped abusive males—husbands or otherwise. From my limited knowledge, such bullies seem to end up as serial abusers.

A taller-than-I-am iron fence encloses the shelter, situated in a residential area in Albuquerque's Northeast Heights. That's one contrast with the Albuquerque Opportunity Center, our converted metal building stuck in a commercial district. There are other differences. Barrett House is a low-lying, modern, faux adobe building. At first glance, it might be taken for a business office. After I drive through the front gate, I notice that the Ghost is gliding over a smoothly paved parking lot, not at all like the rough-pebbled surface at the center.

Because I will be loading the Ghost from the rear, I back into a lined-off visitor's space curbside and head for the office. Inside a glassed-off room, a middle-aged woman camps behind a polished wooden desk. She is decked out in a tailored business suit. No hair dares to wander about on her head. She looks up and waves me in through a second set of doors. The office is painted in pastels and lit by indirect light. All is calm, if not bright. I contrast this with the glare of the overhead fluorescent lighting at the AOC.

"Hi. I'm here to pick up a donation for the Albuquerque Opportunity Center men's shelter." Should I give out my name?

My question is answered. "And you are?"

"Fred Bales. I'm a volunteer down there."

The woman checks a clipboard and then rises to walk into another room. "Just a moment." Befitting her attire, she is all business. Soon she returns with a younger woman, maybe 30, dressed in what would pass for hospital scrubs, pink-colored. She flashes a winning smile.

No introductions are made, but the young woman says, "Follow me."

I thank the gatekeeper and find myself in a shiny-bright hallway leading to a storeroom chock full of bottles and tubes and boxes.

"Well, here it is. By the way, my name is Amy."

"I'm Fred. Thanks for all of this."

"You're welcome to it, but not quite all." She leads me to four boxes, each about three-feet square and maybe a foot-and-a-half tall. "These are yours." She produces a hand truck for transporting our haul.

"Hello, dolly," I say.

Amy laughs, delighting me. I assume that she is one of the sheltered women assigned to on-site chores. She wears lipstick but no other makeup, and shows no bruises or scars on her face or arms, leading me to guess that she has been resident at Barrett House for more than a few days. Then I take a second guess, remembering hearing that abusers often target body blows to their victims so that the effects will be concealed under clothing.

With Amy's help I move outside with the boxes, although they are a bit wide for the hand-truck platform, causing me to tilt the apparatus at a low angle to the floor. My back complains. Two trips suffice. Amy pitches in with piling boxes into the Ghost and bids me a cheery farewell. I wish her the same, hoping with all my heart that she steers clear of harm's way after leaving Barrett House.

Back at the center's store room, sorting occupies about a half hour of placing the donated items into appropriate bins. Some supplies, mini-bottles of shampoo especially, had been depleted.

My customary volunteer hours are almost gone, but curiosity and a sense of obligation compel me to go upstairs before signing out. Jennifer greets me with a wide and sly grin when I ask about other tasks.

"Why, yes, Fred, I'm going to take the bulk mailing down to the Post Office. We didn't get around to it yesterday. I know you're dying to help out."

"You got that right—the dying part, I mean." Still, the thought of girding for battle with Richard, or watching a surrogate do battle, stimulates me in a perverse way, and so I rise to the bait. "Okay, I'll humor you. But you'll have to do all the talking."

The paperwork already is filled out, and we load the Ghost with the mailing. I drive, and on the way ask about the Cardozo book's fate.

"Oh, I forgot to tell you," Jennifer says. "Dennis bought it for his brother who's a lawyer in Indiana. Dennis's going back there this week and will give it to him for a Christmas present."

"What did he pay for it, if you don't mind my asking?"

"Two-hundred-and-fifty dollars."

I gloat. "That seems like poetic justice to me, even though it is prose." I say this as we locate a parking spot outside the bulk mail entrance. So far, so good today: a productive trip to the bank, Joseph's cadging pens, success at Barrett House, and a perfect ending to the rare book saga. I suppose it's nothing less than a pipe dream to anticipate perfection.

We haul our boxes inside and deposit them on a flat-bed cart. Jennifer rolls the assemblage up to the intake desk where she is greeted—that's the correct word—by Richard.

"Hello, how can I help you today?" Can this be Richard speaking?

A few other customers are processing mailings, allowing me to remain in the background with my dingy blue cap tugged low over my forehead. Eavesdropping, I anticipate further developments.

Jennifer submits the form and Richard approves it after a cursory glance. The weighing and stuffing into the prescribed boxes all go without incident.

"Looks like you have a Christmas mailing here," Richard says. "Well, Merry Christmas to you."

Gag me with a kitchen utensil. Richard is coming off as the incarnation of personality plus. You would think he's bucking for Mr. Congeniality at the Mr. America Pageant.

The mailing is stowed and Jennifer signs and picks up a receipt, after which Richard gushes forth a hearty, "Thank you" to Jennifer.

I am left to conjecture whether I was in the same place with the same actors as before. Maybe I have time-traveled without appreciating it. Certainly, Kafka could have spun one of his yarns from my two visits to the bulk mail room. Maybe I'll try writing about it myself, given Kafka's current state.

Grinning from ear to ear as we return to the parking lot, Jennifer inserts a verbal needle under my skin. "See, Fred, you have to know how to handle these guys."

I refuse to take that bait, but I fancy that my sparkling prose to the postmaster and its fallout have culminated in removing a thorn from the sides of bulk-mailing patrons. Who dares deny it?

Chapter ELEVEN

I'm lonesome. I'm steering the Gray Ghost to the Veterans Affairs complex with nary a passenger. The VA hierarchy has decreed that all volunteers visiting their premises undergo a security check entailing finger-printing and the inevitable "official" form. I assume that this exercise represents delayed fallout from the 9/11 attack.

The mandate seems nonsensical to me. No one guards the perimeter of the VA grounds, at least in daytime when I drive in unchallenged, although I have heard that the grounds are patrolled at night. Moreover, no guard ever inhabits the World War II adobe-style structure sitting by the ungated entrance. Truly, all 9/11 bombers and their ilk could march into the grounds *en masse*—not sneak through—on the sidewalk without triggering an alarm. Likewise, an armored personnel carrier could rumble through on the street side without a shot being fired. Besides, we volunteers infrequently step inside any building out there, dropping off and picking up our men outdoors. So, what's the point?

Some volunteers and Jennifer negotiated the security process yesterday, leaving me as the sole supplicant today. "It only took about fifteen minutes," Jennifer has assured me.

I have been directed to report to Building 4, second floor. Building designations in black lettering on turquoise-background signs point the way on winding roadways, and I find Building 4, the elevator, and office without a misstep. Maybe I have been too negative about this appointment.

Inside, a woman with curly red hair greets me at a waist-high counter. When I explain my mission, she asks for my ID.

ID? I tell her that I have no official VA identification, but that I am a volunteer at the Albuquerque Opportunity Center, present and accounted for, and seeking to fill out a form and be fingerprinted.

She discounts that, suggesting that I go next door to the main hospital's basement and consult the folks there about verifying my volunteer home base. She fetches a map and begins to show me the route.

I balk, and not because I know the way blindfolded. "Surely, you have my name on a roster from the center. Some of our folks were out here yesterday."

Either she was not present yesterday or is engaging in gameswomanship because she professes no knowledge of that visit. With some prodding, she exits to check for my name but returns, saying that it does not appear on any list and that she has no manifest for the Albuquerque Opportunity Center.

Why fight city hall? "Tell you what. I'll go back to the AOC office and come back tomorrow with a letter or something to satisfy you."

"Yes, please do that."

Back at the center, I whine to Brian about my wasted sixteen-mile roundtrip. Shaking his head, he is appalled and sympathetic, commenting that he forwarded a list with all our names. He promises to whomp up a letter for me and ring up a VA contact for skid-greasing.

"Thanks, my man," I say in Joseph style.

Having spent more than an hour on my wild paper chase, I seek out Jennifer. She also apologizes about my having to revisit the VA. No pending assignments are scheduled, prompting me to ask about updates on my past riding companions.

"Well," she begins, "Armando got in trouble up in Santa Fe. He lives with his sister now and broke his parole."

"How?"

"He was drinking, which of course is a no-no on parole, and threw a beer can at a car—a police car. He did some jail time."

Given my elapsed time on the planet and at the opportunity center in particular, few events shock me these days, and this darkly humorous report rates accordingly. Tossing a beer can at a police car, indeed. Armando always was a mite impetuous. I ask about one of Armando's former dorm mates. "Ever hear from Luther?"

"Oh, sure. He calls about once a week. He's unhappy." (This qualifies as breaking news, doesn't it?) "He's living with another fellow but wants out. His lone success seems to have been qualifying for Social Security disability."

That rates a cheer. Good for old Luther. Has he worn out his $2,000 shoes?

***

Today I report in and opine to Brian that the VA seems to be setting the agenda for the Albuquerque Opportunity Center. He smiles before printing out an email verifying my status. I notice that the message refers to me as a volunteer for the Metropolitan Homelessness Project. A mental light blinks, dimly. Yes, I should have referred to our parent organization instead of the Albuquerque Opportunity Center on yesterday's mission unaccomplished. Well, maybe.

Armed with two picture IDs and Brian's letter, plus one that Jennifer insisted on writing, I retrace the trek to the VA complex. Just for the record, no one guards the gate, and no guard will be stationed there in my lifetime. You can write it down, as I just did.

Inside Building 4, I board the elevator and push the second-floor button. Having performed this drill yesterday, I allow that this procedure could become second nature. As if to mock my thought, the door begins to slide shut but jarringly retreats, repeating this cycle three times before I give up and ask a passing jean-clad workman for directions to the stairs. He points to a sign less than two feet in front of me. It says "Stairs" with an arrow pointing the way. I laugh and begin my ascent.

Upstairs, a receptionist takes my name, gives my documentation a cursory glance, and hands over a form, directing me to complete it at a metal desk in a shadowy corner. The red-haired woman is nowhere to be seen.

The form seems routine, requiring basic stuff such as name, address, Social Security number, and the like. After I return with the document, a woman who seems to be the junior hire is summoned to take my fingerprints. She greets me cheerfully, and I follow her into a small room where a middle-aged woman is chomping on a burrito. The young woman is friendly, bantering and smiling, but emits the nervous air of someone new to her job.

I repeat to myself that Jennifer has assured me that the procedure two days ago went smoothly, and I anticipate a short visit in the cramped interior room. A scanner sits opposite the burrito-eater. It is mid-morning, and whether she is consuming a late breakfast, or a brunch, or an early lunch, I can't say.

The young woman squirts a liquid onto the scanner's glass top and grips my right hand to press my four finger tips onto the surface. The machine whirs and then beeps. My whorls—as I recall, that's the terminology for the curvy lines embedded at the ends of fingers and thumbs—show up with a smattering of vein-like red traces. This turns out to be a bad sign, indicating that a portion of my prints did not register properly. The young woman pushes ahead, maneuvering both sets of fingers and then the thumbs.

Thank God it's over. Both of us were getting antsy, and the burrito woman had become transfixed with the operation.

"Okay. Now, sir, we need to roll your fingers and thumbs," my hand-holder says.

Blimey. How much longer can this torture go on? I feel awkard as my fingers and thumbs are grasped and then rotated. To accommodate the best position for my hands on the glass, I stand at an awkward angle that is beginning to aggravate my back muscles.

"Try to relax," I am told, squelching the urge to echo the same advice. I feel my fingers slipping sideways during this process. My keeper frowns and wipes the glass before we have another go. The machine beeps after each take. The burrito-chomping woman calls over that my attendant is rolling the fingers too fast. This interjection from a superior does not calm my helper, nor placate me. If our kibitzer knows so much, why doesn't she make her way over and assist?

Fingers are rolled at a slower pace, but spidery

red lines continue to bleed on the fingerprint images. An older woman arrives with another victim and seems annoyed by our presence. She says she is in a hurry. Who isn't? Over my minder's objections the older woman rolls my fingers. She has no more success than the young woman, who has gained my unqualified sympathy. Finally, the burrito woman and the older woman determine that they will override the readouts of my prints and fire them off into bureaucratic cyberspace.

The "boss" has polished off her burrito and approaches me with yet another paper to fill in, verifying that my fingerprints were taken on a certain date. "Send this in with your other paper work." Other paper work? Is Brian cognizant of this?

Earlier, as she checked over my initial form, the "boss" insisted that I list my position as "Contractor." I replied that I was a "Volunteer" and that if I were a "Contractor" I should be receiving a fat paycheck from the Metropolitan Homelessness Project. Considering her silence at my incisive remark, I figured she was the humorless type. But, dash it all, I'm a volunteer, period. I never signed a contract and won't. Veterans Affairs can mangle meaning inside its procedural strait jacket, but I was, am, and always will be a volunteer—and proud to be one. Get over it, VA. Somewhere, George Orwell is laughing or crying—maybe both.

Now the "boss" mentions that if the ruling powers somewhere out there determine that my prints do not meet an acceptable standard, I will be required to have them retaken.

At that prospect I remain mute but begin plotting my resistance movement to the whole beeping and bleeping process.

Back at the center, I announce that I will boycott any further finger-printing, noting that if I am banished from the VA's premises I still could haul clothes and stuff to St. Martin's, Goodwill, or Thrift Town, monitor the library, accompany Al to Home Depot, drive men to the University Hospital and Health Care for the Homeless, and perform general errands. "Let me see Big Brother stop me," I conclude with a flourish of my hands.

Brian smiles. My outbursts invariably amuse him. Anew, I consider the stereotype of young people as radical and unforgiving types, and question why Brian and Jennifer appear to roll with the punches while Mr. Three-Score-and-Ten-With-Time-To-Spare gets himself into a tizzy over minor annoyances spawned by bureaucracies running amok.

Overcoming my inflated sense of self-importance, I register an internal reminder that issues other than salving my ego take priority at the center. As proof, the telephone rings. After talking briefly, Brian forwards the call to Jennifer. Brian informs me that the caller was a city worker, claiming that the center failed to pay an operating license fee. "We have the check that we paid," he comments nonchalantly.

I am consoled by knowing that I am not alone in encountering a clumsy bureaucracy. Yet, that news sets me off again with poor Brian on the receiving end. "What kind of background check is required for a life-long American who never held citizenship in any other country, possesses a valid passport, was finger-printed for Peace Corps service—which I bet my boots is buried in a file in Washington—who worked for the state of New Mexico and the state of Texas as a teacher, and has only two moving vehicle violations on his police record?

All of this bother is making me begin to doubt my identity. Who am I, anyway?"

"I assume that's a rhetorical question, Freddy." Brian does have a way of bringing my hot air balloon crashing to earth.

The finger-printing recalls Peace Corps days. Our training group was brought to the local police station to have our prints taken the old-fashioned way, in goopy ink. I have a tendency toward sweaty hands, and some poor devil had to wrestle with my fingers during three separate visits before registering a decent set of prints. The young fellow who provided rides for us then—a job not unlike mine now at the AOC—was a convivial grad student whose name is unremembered. When this amiable fellow drove me to my third go-around at the police station, he harkened to the Dick Tracy comic strip and the assorted characters with nicknames reflecting outlandish physical characteristics. He commented that I would be dubbed "Sweaty Fingers" in that strip. That strikes me as funny now. I hope it did then.

"Speaking of questions, Brian, a woman at the VA said something about having to do an online form. She was kidding, right?"

Brian's Buddha smile emerges. "No worry. I'll help you with it."

Going through my oft-practiced ritual, I am not praying despite letting loose with language associated with that activity.

Back home, after Brian forwards the form to me via email, I struggle with the cyber questionnaire, not because the questions are difficult but because glitches occur when I try to move to the next box or page or, worse, try to back up. This is painfully problematic when listing my employment experiences, in reverse order. Editing the form, I discover that I left out one location. The form refuses to allow me to reverse gears to make the addition, and I note that I am allowing this inanimate image on a computer screen to assume anthropomorphic dimensions. I have been had.

At the bottom of the form, I indulge myself by commenting in a box intended for open-ended remarks. Within that space I type, "Orwell would be proud of you."

I have completed the "thing" as best I could and email it to Brian. I assume he will clean it up for me before delivering it into the bowels of the federal bureaucracy. Maybe it will meet up with my fingerprints there. Upon reflection I would have been closer to the intended mark to have written, "Kafka would be proud of you." That sentiment would come closer to approximating my assessment of this rat-maze experiment, but it's too late to update my response now.

During his fifteen-plus minutes of fame on the presidential campaign trail, George Wallace promised, if elected, to visit every government office and count off every fourth desk to inform the occupant that he or she would need to seek employment elsewhere. I considered that a hare-brained proposal at the time and still do, although my position is weakening.

Calming down, I have a third thought. Bureaucracies by and large are established for logical purposes and staffed by well-meaning men and women. But at the operational level bureaucrats are hamstrung at times by rules from above that make sense in the aggregate but are inane in the particular. Or, maybe I'm the one being too particular—or inane.

Chapter TWELVE

I admit it. I asked for it. And I got it. What I got was an email today from Veterans Affairs rejecting my security application. As an added insult, the cyberspace fellow who reviewed my online form was not at all taken with my allusion to George Orwell.

The forwarded message reads:

Subject: Rejected E-QIP
August 19, 2011

Dear Frederick Bales,

Your investigative questionnaire, request number 9926575, has been reviewed. As a result of this review, this request has been rejected because of the following:
Your E-QIP is being rejected. Please log back into E-QIP and correct the following items:
Section 1: Full Name
Please provide your full first and middle names
Section 9: Where you went to school
Please remove the additional comments and report the complete address for University of Texas Registrar Office
Section 10: Your Employment Activities
Please report full name for your verifier of unemployment periods

Additional Comments at the end of the E-QIP
Please remove "Orwell would be proud of you"
    You will need to print off, sign, and return the new
E-QIP signature pages, as well as, the attached OF-306
form. Please return them via email/fax (see signature block).
    Also, your fingerprints were captured on March 17,
2011, and per OPM policy, finger prints are only good for
120 days. The fingerprints expired on July 17, 2011.
    Please use the attached National List of VA finger-
print stations to schedule an appointment with your nearest
VA facility to have your fingerprints electronically captured
again for submission to OPM. Also, bring the attached SAC
Memorandum with you for that VA-PIV stations processing.
    Your access to the Electronic Questionnaires for Inves-
tigations Processing (e-QIP) has been re-activated at http://
www.opm.gov/e-QIP so that you can modify your data and
re-submit it. You must answer some yes/no questions again
because the information may have changed since you last re-
sponded. Please modify your data as appropriate, certify and
release your form as soon as possible to expedite processing.

    Sincerely,

    Byron Fox
    Department of Veterans Affairs
    Personnel Security Specialist

    Harrumph. I have said before and I repeat now
for those not subjected to my original pronouncement:
What this country needs is a good dose of humor. Perhaps I should give our public servants a second chance.
For instance, what might my reviewer say if I indeed sub-
stitute Kafka for Orwell on the next go-around? If Mr.

Fox is still on the prowl, I already have my answer.

I struggle with the meanings of OPM, SAC and PIV, although I can figure out that VA stands for Veterans Affairs—I think. Other than the acronyms, the communiqué's meaning is perfectly clear, to borrow a Richard Nixon expression.

It is clear that I am being required to have my fingerprints taken over in part because they "are only good for 120 days." This has caused me to examine my fingertips more than once since receiving the rejection. Have I grown new whorls, or have the old ones expanded or contracted, or what? And I must raise the skeptic's age-old nitpick: Why not 119 days or 121 days?

Annoyingly, I plead guilty as charged to not typing in my middle name, using my middle initial instead of the full "Vincent." Ever vigilant in these matters to expose inconsistencies, I checked my passport. Alas, my complete middle name appears there, meaning that the national security apparatus is aligned on that requirement and rates one point on the scoreboard—to replace the zero.

At the center today, I am waylaid by the homelessness project director, Dennis Plummer. He refers to his copy of my rejection notice and guffaws at the reference to Orwell. "That's truly funny, Fred. Good luck with the VA."

"To tell you the truth, I'm balking on reapplying. And if I did, I'm just ornery enough to write in Kafka for Orwell. Sorry if this causes you problems."

"No, don't worry about it. Do what you want to. Anyway, I promise to come and visit you in prison."

Dennis's making light of my windmill-tilting exercise reinforces my affection for the staff I work with here, an assessment that just jumped up another peg. Truly, I don't want to create waves for the homelessness agency, least of all for Dennis who has enough legitimate outside business to attend to without having to clean up after a wise-guy volunteer. Yet, as the revered philosopher Popeye was prone to say, "I yam what I yam."

In fact, this ordeal transcends a tempest in a teapot because it goes to the heart of the First Amendment. In a reputed free country, why can't I make a statement to my government about Orwellian/Kafkaesque goings-on? Don't I have the right to tweak the beard of the bureaucratic lion, who in the flesh is my employee and that of fellow taxpayers? This bothersome episode evokes Ben Franklin's enduring aphorism, stating something to the effect that a people who trade liberty for security deserve neither.

Let me be perfectly clear: When and if the Veterans Affairs secures its perimeter at the local complex and posts a guard at the main entrance, I will be first in line to complete a revised form and submit my expired fingerprints for rescanning. Honest.

Meantime, a new man, Nelson, has signed up to ride so that he can hand-carry an application to the city's housing office. A man I don't recognize rests on the couch when I descend the stairs into respite. By elimination, I assume that the fellow on the couch is Nelson, a conjecture confirmed when we introduce ourselves. Outside, he piles into the shotgun seat but shuns conversation while I concentrate on driving to the housing office, a place where I have sat with many a man in a prototype "take-a-number" or "hear-a-name" waiting room. I pull up outside the office's main entrance and drop Nelson before jockeying for a parking spot.

After nosing out an aggressive contender for a space, I go inside where Nelson is awaiting his turn to see a case worker. He sports a white beard that contrasts with his sandy-colored hair. In a voice that carries the hint of a British accent and a man approaching—or arrived at—retirement age, he asks me to hold his place so that he can slip outside for a smoke.

Five minutes after returning, Nelson is called. I shadow him into an office where a woman who appears to be not far beyond traditional college age greets us. I explain my role as she pulls Nelson's jacket from a file cabinet. Her desk is cluttered, implying that she is overworked. I'll remember that if we land in Orwell/Kafka territory.

Nelson produces the forms filled out with Jennifer's help.

The woman scans the paperwork. "Okay, this looks pretty good, Nelson, but you need you to obtain a copy of your divorce decree for me."

Nelson shakes his head. "That was twenty-eight years ago down in El Paso. I don't even know if my ex is still alive."

"What we need is the official copy of the divorce, that's all."

I butt in. "Aren't these things online nowadays?"

The case worker seems to appreciate my deflecting Nelson's focus from her. "Some are, that's right. But his divorce was so long ago that it probably hasn't been scanned in."

Nelson stands and I follow, straining for an exit line. "Maybe Jennifer or Brian can help out with this."

"I hope so," Nelson says in a voice carrying a white-flag tone. He turns to the woman behind the desk. "Thanks for getting me this far. I'll try and check on the decree, or whatever."

On the way to the Ghost I mull over the divorce-decree requirement, concluding that it makes sense. I can picture couples promoting a scam whereby one fronts for public housing and then arranges for the spouse to sneak in. Who checks for these potential violations?

Inside the van, sounds blare from the radio speakers when I turn the ignition key. My taste for country music is not shared by my wife, so I tune into country classics when wheeling around town alone. To promote conversation, I don't play the radio when I'm with the men, and I move to punch the power button.

Nelson intervenes. "Leave it on. That music brings back memories of El Paso."

I ask about El Paso and the incongruous British accent.

"I grew up in Mexico, actually. My dad was a British mining engineer and my mother was Mexican. We spoke English mostly around the house, but I picked up a lot of Spanish as well. It was a good boyhood for me, especially the way things are now with bilingualism all the rage."

"And then you got to El Paso."

"My parents moved there and I went along because I was ready for college. I lasted two years at U-TEP before flunking out."

"What happened?"

"I got over-involved in a fraternity."

Given past histories and an educated stab at Nelson's age, I bet the house on what will come next.

"Then I got drafted and went to Vietnam. That's when I got into drugs. Nobody should have gone to Vietnam, that's for sure. You over there?"

"No, I missed it. Between graduate school and

the Peace Corps I ended up being old enough to finesse the draft." What a word, "finesse." Let's not mince words here. I and most others of my class flat-out avoided the draft. Why can't I say the word "ducked"?

"You're a lucky man. No need to apologize for it. Anyway, all those bad habits I picked up in Nam cost me a good job or two, and a wife over the years. So here I am in scenic Albuquerque."

We have foundered on what cliché-mongers describe as "a pregnant pause." I try to concentrate on the undercurrent of country music. Waylon Jennings is holding forth with "Good Hearted Woman."

"Know who wrote that one?" Nelson asks.

Bless him for breaking new ice. "Can't say that I do."

"Willie Nelson."

With the conversation shifted into less sensitive territory, I venture an amateur critic's opinion that of Willie's three talents, songwriting would rank first, followed in order by guitar-playing and singing.

"Most people, me included, would agree with you on that, Fred."

Nelson and I have reached an accommodation, and I have reached the outer boundaries of my knowledge of county singers and songwriters.

We listen to more music, Nelson commenting about singers and songs, before we are treated to John Conlee's "Common Man." Nelson chimes in on the chorus.

I'm just a common man, drive a common van.
My dog ain't got no pedigree.

"I don't consider myself a common man, do you, Nelson?"

"No, I don't. But who does?"

Now there's a rhetorical question for you, Fred. No individual on God's green earth should be considered common. As for the common van, I'll stick up for the Ghost, whose odometer is pressing 189,000 miles, the majority spent in service to humanity. Common, indeed. Besides, I don't own a dog. John Conlee, or whoever wrote the lyrics, had some other character in mind as the subject of that number. That's perfectly clear.

Chapter THIRTEEN

Shave 20 years off Rob's life and he could grace a U.S. Army recruiting poster. I can visualize a colored-picture likeness—accentuated by even features, blue eyes, and wavy brown hair—staring out at military wannabes, the subtext cooing to them, "You, too, can enjoy a glamorous future in service to your country."

Nowadays, Rob exemplifies clean-cut—no beard and neatly combed hair held in place by a fragrant topping. Before joining him for his ride, I learned that he tends to talk almost non-stop. "Hyper" was Jennifer's adjective. I am familiar with the type. Bring him on.

We will be visiting the VA two days before Christmas. I'm in a good mood despite a sustained cold snap with sub-freezing temperatures overnight and sub-40-degree days. Again, I note that these readings may not impress denizens of International Falls, but they signify abnormality in Albuquerque.

When I meet Rob, he wears no outer jacket. I take notice and say so.

"Don't worry. I've got a good one in storage that I'll pick up today at the VA. I don't like the cold at all."

This admission comes as a relief because I feared that Rob was pledged to that goofy band of macho men around town who wear T-shirts and nothing but T-shirts above their waists in wintertime. Hewing to the subject, I mention reading that the Northeast U.S. endured a major weekend snowstorm.

"Yeah, I read about that, too. I don't see how those people live back there. They've always been there, I guess."

I tell Rob about my pledge taken many years ago to avoid living north of I-40. He agrees with that, and gives out an appreciative laugh when I tell him that when my wife and I returned to Albuquerque from New Orleans we bought a house one mile north of that interstate. The fates will have their little joke, won't they?

Now that we're aligned on the subject of cold-weather and we're on the road, I ask Rob about his health. I understood that he was knifed.

"I was in the DOM at the VA, and ...."

I cut in. "Help me out here. What's the DOM?"

"Oh, yeah, sorry. DOM stands for a domiciliary residential program. It's a live-in rehab deal with a bunch of counseling about how to keep vets from going back on the streets. There's a drug-rehab part, too, and a work-therapy part."

I let Rob's involvement with the ins and outs of that program await another ride on another day. And despite my security background check farce, I must laud the Veterans Affairs for offering a range of programs for its namesakes. How well these programs are operated or how many potential beneficiaries fall between the cracks, I cannot say.

"When I got knifed I was just a couple of blocks from the VA. I had this blue bag with some of my stuff in it and this guy came at me. He got part of my stomach and lung, and I lost my spleen and part of my pancreas. It's growing back now. I still got a tube draining my stomach."

I'm impressed. When we reach a red light, Rob lifts his shirt to unveil an aspirin-sized bottle attached to a tube protruding from his lower left abdomen. I'm impressed even more. "Did you pass out?"

"Nah, I was able to start walking to Gibson to get some help when this cop saw me and pulled over. The emergency guys took me to UNMH. They got the best trauma unit up there, and then I was in the ER and right away to the OR. They patched me up."

Like many veterans I have known, Rob sprinkles his conversation with acronyms. These three I can keep up with, however, unlike the runes in my security clearance rejection.

"I was doing good, too. I had a place to stay here and a job. I was saving money and getting my act together. I guess bad things happen to good people."

I fear we are making twenty-five knots for deep-water, and I am unprepared and unqualified for a seminar on why bad things happen to good people and the subtleties attached to that imponderable. Although I remember reading a book by that title, I opt for the path of least resistance. "I'm afraid so. I guess there's that random part of life where something or someone comes down on you no matter whether you're a saint or a sinner." I tack on the old Biblical verse. "The rain falls on the just and unjust alike." I make a mental note to double check the context of that one.

My response seems to satisfy Rob, and heaven knows getting off with that pithy line of cracker-barrel philosophy satisfies me. I ask about what he was doing out in the first place.

"I was heading back from seeing a buddy over in that neighborhood. He was on probation, but after I got there I found out he was drinking and carrying on. I don't need that, believe me. I got out of there, man."

Good move, albeit bad timing. I sympathize with what can be best cataloged as bad luck, and move on to a favorite evergreen question, service experience.

"I was in the Army special forces—1979 to 1983. I got in between all the wars, except for Granada. I came out okay, but a buddy of mine got it. We dropped from 500 feet and he got shot in the air. It was supposed to be a secure LZ but it wasn't."

"LZ?"

"Landing Zone. It wasn't much bigger than that lot over there." Rob gestures toward a patch of land adjoining the road. "He took a round just under his flak jacket." Rob points to the center of his waist. "Some Commie got him, a tracer bullet. They were using the same ammo as us in their AK-47s, and the bullet spun inside him and tore him up. He was dead when he hit the ground." Rob gazes into the distance. "It was tough to leave him there, but we had to do the mission. They did a 'bag-and-tag' on him and flew his body back to the states. I never liked that term, 'bag-and-tag.'"

I never did either.

"I was in some firefights when we went house-to-house, but it wasn't much. The thing is, you don't know who you're shooting then. Civilians are around, women and children, and you hope you don't get them in the crossfire."

Rob warms to the topic of geopolitics. "I don't know why those people want to mess with us. We're the most powerful nation on earth. They're just going to get wiped out. Saddam Hussein. We got his ass."

I answer by opining that logic on our terms doesn't appear to underlie terrorists' activities, adding that these characters seem to be driven by rigid ideology.

"Ideology? Call it what you want, but they're going down. Take the Navy Seals. They're all over the place. They're over there in the Mideast right now as civilians. They're doing recon but they look like civilians."

Rob's appointment is in Building 1, the VA's old main hospital transformed into a psychology unit, among other uses. As I park, we discuss his getting back to the center and finding a ride to University Hospital on Saturdays when staff and drivers are scarce. I advise a consultation with Jennifer. "I know it's tough on Saturday. But I think there's a shuttle. She'll know. Anyway, it's good to talk with you, Rob. You be around next week?"

"Oh, yeah. They say I'll be stuck for three weeks at least, until I can get the tube out of my side."

"See you then, probably Wednesday." I look forward to our next seminar. Rob is brim full of entertaining tales and provocative ideas.

***

It's Thursday and a new Rob, plus Norman and Carl, both companions from yesterday, are on the ride list. I collect them in respite, but not before Rob the First asks to tag along to the VA despite neglecting to sign up.

Sure. Who am I of all people to become a by-the-book bureaucrat? Besides, I wanted to see him again.

Four passengers ensure that I will drive a white whale transport van, one of the imposing "Mobies." But the big van would have been the choice regardless because when I boarded the Gray Ghost earlier, my knees caressed my chin. I arched my back and tried to jam the seat back but it failed to budge. Checking behind the headrest, I came face to face with two compartment-length cardboard boxes crammed into the space.

Upstairs to retrieve the white van key, I asked Jennifer about the load. "Oh, I forgot. We got a donation of sheets and blankets and a mattress that we'll use for furnishing an apartment for a guy moving out. No need to unload that stuff and then reload it."

Agreed, and I predict that I will be summoned for that work detail.

Outside respite the four of us wait for Norman. Rob the First evidences an intolerant side, speaking about Norman. "He sleeps next to me and he talks all the time. Talk, talk, talk. I finally told him to get lost and quit bothering me." The others signal assent. And in my time with Norman to and from his radiation treatment yesterday, he exercised his mouth nonstop.

I go inside and find Norman engaged on the telephone. I approach him so he cannot escape seeing me and gesture toward the door. No sooner has he hung up than Jennifer walks by and he strikes up a conversation with her. I press the issue and Norman dons a baseball cap at a jaunty angle and trails me out the door.

Inside the van, Carl sits next to me, head lowered and clutched between his hands. Depression? Norman claims the back bench seat alone, with the two Robs in the seat behind me. Between Rob the First and Norman, I predict that Norman will initiate the conversation. On cue, Norman comments that he carries a coupon to pick up a Christmas turkey at the VA.

The others pooh-pooh that by uttering a chorus of guttural sounds. Keeping his head lowered, Carl adds words. "Even if you get a turkey, which seems like a long shot, what are you going to do with it, anyway?"

Good question. No cooking facilities besides a

microwave grace the center. But a turkey is a turkey, I suppose. Maybe a staff member could tote the bird home and return it ready to eat.

Norman must be cowed by the skeptics because Rob the Second takes the floor to fill me in on his plight. He is scheduled in at Presbyterian Hospital to pick up meds and finish paperwork. I catch on to the fact that he suffered a ruptured esophagus and since then has encountered one medical obstacle after another. With deep-set eyes and long blond hair pulled away from his forehead, this Rob could pass for the twin brother of the late actor Lloyd Bridges.

Rob the First, showing another example of intolerance, orders Rob the Second to cease and desist. "Nobody wants to hear about your problems." I realize that his bunk mates have been cooped up long enough, two or three days, to have heard their new cohort's tale of woe to the exhaustion point.

My charges fall silent. I am at a stoplight and inch forward to read a bumper sticker on the car ahead. "Practice Random Acts of Scratching," it says, prompting remembrances of the center's bedbug infestation.

I drop Rob the Second at Presbyterian after forgetting that I was piloting a sluggish Moby rather than the Ghost. This lapse caused me to gun the van into the left lane to dodge a slow poke backing up traffic in Central's curb lane. The top-heavy van swayed conspicuously in the process, and I heard a "Way to go, Fred" from Norman. Other accolades poured in after my burst of derring-do, compliments seldom heard about my driving talents.

At the VA, I leave Carl and Rob the First at the main hospital. Norman directs me to Building 1, marked out front by a towering flag pole. Norman is brimming with anticipation, explaining that he won a turkey in a veterans' lottery. As directed by Jennifer, I tell him to go in and ask at the reception desk for Office 5. Instead, he approaches a fellow on the sidewalk, who from my vantage point gives Norman short shrift.

I keep the whale parked hard by the curb in a fire lane, figuring I can move if the gendarmes, or a fire, so demand. I settle in for a long wait and turn to the country classics station. Befitting the season, Christmas numbers are being interspersed with regular tunes. Squeezed in between the genuine classics of George Jones' "He Stopped Loving Her Today," and Emmylou Harris' "Together Again," I am assailed by "Leroy the Redneck Reindeer." That's a classic? If so, the end is near. Culturally, "Leroy" ranks right up there with deep-fried Twinkies in my book. And the song can't begin to measure up to a classy classic title such as "Old Flames Can't Hold a Candle to You."

Despite widespread doubts from his compatriots about his mission, a smiling Norman emerges within ten minutes holding a whopping turkey in one hand and a sack of unpopped popcorn in the other. I help load the turkey, which must weigh twenty-five pounds—frozen solid, naturally. Norman and I speculate what will be done with it at the center.

"I'll think of something," Norman says.

We wend our way back to the main hospital to check on Carl and Rob the First, who predicted short stays. On the way, Norman allows that he wouldn't mind going in and picking up his meds. Uh-oh. This situation is shaping up like the old joke about the guy on a tour bus who volunteered to search for a tardy traveler.

"Do you want me to look for Joe?" he asks. And the tour director replies, "No, because I don't want to have to go looking for you." Point well taken.

We stop and Norman steps down, but rather than angling toward the entrance he hobbles toward a fellow stationed across the driveway. Bless Bess, it's a former resident, William, who decamped from the center last week. William wears a lanyard with a plastic badge dangling from the bottom. He and Norman talk animatedly for a minute before William comes over and opens the passenger-side door. He informs me that he will be taking possession of the turkey. What? What can I say? It's Norman's turkey to relinquish, I admit. I look toward the hospital entrance and spot Norman beaming back at us in approval. I hope he has cut a deal to share a meal with William and other hangers-on.

I ask William if he has a job at the VA. He nods. "I'm making nine dollars an hour." He is nowhere to be seen in the parking area, however, after he makes off with the turkey.

A van in front of the whale has pulled away and a taxi replaces it. Its left rear door opens and a yellowish, wooden cane appears, followed by two feet, and at last the head and torso of a white-haired man. He moves deliberately, standing precariously before closing the door and taking baby steps around the taxi's rear in rhythm with the cane's movements. As he passes before me I notice that his royal-blue baseball cap bears in gold letters, "Vietnam Veteran." Why must he take a taxi for medical treatment? Will he be reimbursed?

Norman is hitting on all cylinders. Within the playing of three country songs, accompanied by the obligatory wind from the DJ, Norman pulls himself into the van with his meds, including 320 pills of some-thing-or-other to be taken "every six hours as needed," as he informs me, plus pain killers. "I really need those," he says of the pain killers. Also, he has secured bandages for an open wound aggravated by radiation.

I ask about the turkey's destination.

"Oh, William is going to give it to a single moth-er that he knows. She has two kids. I figured she needed it more than I do."

No comment. But shame on me for imitating Doubting Thomas.

Norman reports that he spotted Carl inside in the waiting area, spurring hopes that I will hit the shut-tle jackpot and have Carl and Rob the First on board within a few minutes. Those minutes and more elapse before Rob appears. "We're going to be another two hours, so go on."

This is Rob's last day with us. He has informed me that he will be traveling to Los Angeles with "a friend." I ask about winter driving conditions. "Oh, no, we're taking the train."

Interesting. I bid Rob the First Godspeed and we shake hands.

Before closing the door, he says, "You guys never let me down and I appreciate that." He hesitates before adding, "You're a good man, Fred."

Who says I don't get paid in this job?

Chapter FOURTEEN

My schedule stays on track at Presbyterian Hospital where Rob the Second paces outside. He sits shotgun on the return to the center, illuminating details surrounding his losing skirmish with a bologna sandwich. He was chomping away at a spot in the East Mountains when a chunk of the meat caught in his throat. He tried to dislodge the mass with a gulp of water, but the pressure ruptured his esophagus, and in rapid order he found himself flat on his back and air-lifted to Presbyterian Hospital.

As he relates this scenario, I am tempted to proclaim that now I have heard everything. But recent respite experiences caution me to put off bragging rights.

Rob talks at length about his "partner" in real estate development who corralled Rob's belongings and donated them to Goodwill. "That's what he told me. He also got rid of my list of contacts and everything. I'm going to see a lawyer—there's this *pro bono* one—and see if I can nail that damn crook for fraud. He owes me fifteen hundred dollars." Also, the hospital lost his medical records, Rob says. And after he was patched up, "They kicked me out on the streets. Said my insurance was up. Now I'm on the wait list for a bed at their rehab center. Anyhow, I'm at the AOC and glad to be there."

At home base, I recount the morning's events to Jennifer. She is as dumbfounded as I by Norman's turkey giveaway, but concurs that it was his option, a real life single mother or no. Also, I report that the other men have complained that Rob the Second can't get past his oddball health incident. For Jennifer, this tidbit ranks right up there with reporting that the sun rises in the east.

Commenting on Rob the First's train trip to California, Jennifer enlightens me about the "friend" Rob cited as a traveling companion: today's head-down rider, Carl. Heavens to Murgatroyd. Despite headwinds against the journey's success, I abide with them in spirit and lecture myself that I am not the appointed guardian for Rob or Carl or any respite man. Yet my busybody angel camps on my shoulder wishing that Rob the First had hung around long enough to complete his VA domiciliary program.

***

I find Norman being bandaged by Jennifer in the respite unit. He sits in a straight chair while she finishes up the salving, then the placing of two, six-inch-square bandages on his right shoulder and back. I glimpse enough of the open sore to appreciate what Norman endures in radiation. The wound brings to mind the familiar analogy to "hamburger." Jennifer's final touch necessitates uncoiling an elastic bandage to encircle Norman's chest and back.

"Thank you, honey," Norman says.

A near-capacity load has signed up for rides. Besides Norman's daily visit to the University of New Mexico Cancer Center, Rob the Second and his new running mate, Jim, are to visit the state Work Force center to check online for jobs. An unshaven man with Coke-bottle-thick glasses piles in, too. I ask where he wants to go but hear no response.

Norman speaks for him. "He wants to go to one of those motels up the street where he can stay. He's leaving from the bus station at three-thirty tomorrow morning and wants to get to a place where he can catch a taxi to get down there."

I head up the road toward the two designated motels, a short distance beyond the I-25 overpass. At a red light I have positioned the white van in the far left lane when I receive revised orders from Norman.

"Actually, he says he wants to go to Motel 6 down on University." I am impressed with whatever brand of extrasensory perception Norman conjures to communicate with this taciturn fellow.

Glancing in the rearview mirror, I see no cars behind me and undertake a switch to the far right lane where I can negotiate a turn onto University. As I back up to clear the vehicle next door, I hear a blast from a car horn. Oops. Didn't see that compact sitting behind me. For once I appreciate being honked at and slam on the brakes. I make a mental note to adjust the van's mirrors. After the light changes, I zoom on through the intersection and execute a more appropriate tactic, a daring U-turn. No problem, although I wonder what Joseph would say. We get back on track and at Motel 6 drop the quiet man, who rallies long enough to thank me for the lift.

On the way to Norman's treatment, the subject turns to drink, chosen because our just-departed passenger is said to suffer that dependency.

"Getting drunk is stupid," Jim says. "It's one thing to go out and have a few beers and good conversation and good times, but to get drunk sucks. I knew this guy next door where I used to live in Oregon, and he was one of these baby-boomer types who did things to extreme. So, one day he suggests we go out drinking and I knew what that meant. So I told him, 'Sure, let's go out and drink 'til we're silly and then puke all over our shoes. That's a great idea.'"

Norman shares a war story. "You're right, but things was different when we was younger. I remember one time on New Year's Eve when I was drinking beer and some guy gave me a big glass of Boone's apple wine. I chugged it down, and before I knew it I had my stomach cleaned out real good."

I'm starting to turn green around the gills, perhaps remembering some best-sequestered transgressions from my own youth. Let it be recorded, however, that I never tasted Boone's wine, apple or otherwise.

Norman is let off, and as I watch him plod to the cancer center door I remember his bandaging ordeal. Whatever I can do for Norman, I'll do—gladly.

Jim needs to pick up medicine at the VA before he and Rob the Second settle in at Work Force. We play "where-are-you-from," and when I say Indiana, Jim brings up an unsavory tidbit from my home state's past.

"It always amazed me that as far north as Indiana is, it was a hotbed for the Ku Klux Klan. That never made sense to me."

"Me either. That's strange for sure, isn't it?" That will constitute as my lone observation. I could—but won't—cite one estimate that twenty percent of the white male population residing in my home county belonged to the Klan in the 1920s. I also could belabor the obvious that racism knows no geographical boundaries.

Jim salvages some honor for my birth state by invoking an invidious comparison. "You know something else? When I lived in Oregon I learned that way back

Oregon had the highest percentage of Klan membership in the country."

I question that one. "I always pictured Oregon as this big-time progressive state."

"It is now, but not then."

Jim promises a short stop at the VA. Rob the Second and I stay in the van where I ask about the status of his esophagus.

"It's coming along real fine. As long as I take my painkillers, I can take full breaths. But when they wear off, I can only take half breaths because of the pain from where they cut me open." He points to his left side. "They went in here and cut through the muscle and rib cage to get at the windpipe and lungs. I even had bits of bologna in my lungs, if you can imagine."

I prefer to hold my imagination in check, but playfully consider applying for a residency in surgery after all the clinical descriptions I have absorbed, courtesy of my respite men. I ask about the circumstances of Rob's unfinished meal. "Did you make that sandwich?"

"No, some guy handed it to me. And the bologna was this thick." Rob holds up a thumb and forefinger, separated by a half-inch gap. "So I was chewing and chewing on that stuff and decided to force it down. Big mistake. Guess I'm lucky to be alive."

Jim returns with a bag full of pills. He examines one bottle and complains that he ordered ibuprofen but came away with aspirin instead. Likewise, he expresses dissatisfaction with another of his meds—Cialis substituted for Viagra.

Rob is familiar with one of those wonder drugs. "I was with this guy over in Texas and looking for work. And he knew some lab tech who was in on a clinical trial. It paid good money and when I went to apply, I asked what the drug was and they said, 'Viagra.' I was all for that. But when I went in to get checked my blood pressure was off the charts, so I didn't make the trial. Guess I was excited or something about my prospects because I never have high blood pressure. Never."

As I chauffeur this dynamic duo to Work Force, I am party to joking—some clever and some not so clever—about Viagra and the circumstances for its use and close encounters and so on. No doubt about it, my clinical education has assumed a new dimension.

At the state office, both men strain to step out of the white whale, triggering my growing mental shopping list that includes a booster stool for this vehicle. The Ghost is more accommodating because it sits close to the ground, but it remains stranded in Los Lunas, awaiting rescue after undergoing repairs.

Picking up Norman goes perfectly. (Such things happen.) I wait less than five minutes inside before he emerges from radiation. I ask about his back.

"Oh, it's not too bad. And this all could have been worse, you know. At first they thought I had melanoma but it turned out to be basal cell."

Norman is growing on me. He doggedly accepts his lot, and despite his loquaciousness has proved to be a welcome sidekick.

"So how many more treatments, Norman?"

"Let's see. This is my second week and they told me it would be five weeks, thirty-three treatments. I don't go in on weekends."

Norman asks to make a Walmart trip. "It's my birthday and I need to cash a check."

I berate myself. Jennifer informed me about the birthday but I forgot. I wish Norman a belated greeting.

He tells me he wants to use part of the check proceeds to buy Jennifer a present, a stuffed animal. This solidifies Norman's standing with me. Anybody with cancer who considers buying someone else a present on his own birthday merits a gold star on my honor roll.

I park beside the store entrance until shooed away by a security guard. I creep into a space within sight of the entrance. Time goes by but no Norman. I leave the van and meet up with him on his way out.

"I got hung up over there at check-cashing. The machine went down. I think the guy punched a wrong button. Anyway, they had to bring in a supervisor to get the computer up again."

Ever more, I am convinced that the Luddites were on to something.

Norman says he will wait to buy Jennifer's present, but as an alternative seeks one more port of call. "Can we go over to Mickey D's? I want to get me some breakfast, and I'll get one for Jennifer too. You want one, Fred?

"No thanks. I'm fine."

I am taken with Norman's slang reference to McDonald's. He was making a major leap of faith, assuming that I could tumble to the term "Mickey D's." If I ever were a hipster, I'm not one now. Confirmation of that came last fall when I failed to recognize by name even one singing group or singer lined up for concerts at the state fair. In truth, that realization dawned back a few years when my wife persuaded me to accompany her to a Bob Dylan concert, and I much preferred the warm-up act, Merle Haggard. And as far as I'm concerned, Arrowsmith is a novel by Sinclair Lewis, although I believe the band goes by a different spelling. I'm not at all sure about that and don't care to find out. Someone else can look that up. I long to turn on the country classics station as we cruise through Mickey D's drive-thru, but settle for Norman's monologue as entertainment.

Rounding out the morning, I drop my keys into the second-floor wall box and check out with Jennifer, telling her that Norman has a breakfast for her and is set on presenting her with a stuffed animal.

She smiles and shakes her head. "I told him not to do that, but he wants to. He's really a sweet guy."

Indeed.

***

Norman and Tom, a new man, along with Jim and Rob the Second, are loaded into the multiple-passenger Moby today. The Ghost still languishes in Los Lunas, but again could not house five passengers anyway.

Rob and Jim are returning to Work Force. I ask Rob why he was bent over yesterday after he left the van. "Barfing," he tells me. "Something got to me."

Tom, who wears a U.S. Air Force Jacket, has requested a trip to Bank of America for a debit card and then to Walmart for a phone card.

Norman is along for the ride. "I've got to get out of here. I'm going stir crazy." He and anyone else feeling that impulse have my eternal sympathy.

Norman was set for another radiation treatment but the "machine" at University of New Mexico's Cancer Center is broken. I hold my tongue when I hear this. I'm trying to be more tolerant of breakdowns, malfunctions, postponements, cancellations, detours, water main breaks, lane closures, untimed traffic lights, recalls, unannounced closings, power outages, computer crashes, phone trees, restrooms being cleaned, elevators being serviced, check-out lanes closed, and all-around ill-timed annoyances—and, lest I forget, operator error. Despite best intentions, this overdue initiative is taxing my fabled patience.

The whale's passenger compartment becomes stereophonic. Norman repeats news of the radiation machine's breakdown and his postponed appointment to Rob and Jim. Meanwhile, Tom is filling me in about his Air Force service time as I relate it to a high school classmate who flew helicopters in Vietnam. All goes well until Norman turns in my direction and starts in. I'm taking it in both ears, so to speak.

During these conversations, I become distracted and end up blocks on the far side of Work Force. I wheel around in the general direction and plunge us into a residential area, Martineztown, with its winding streets resembling alleys. I put the best face on it. "All aboard for Fred's tour of Martineztown."

An Albuquerque native, Tom knows the territory and we talk about the culture of this venerable and community-minded Hispanic neighborhood. Not to be left out, Rob misdirects our discussion by noting that Santa Fe is the oldest state capital.

With minimal detours we arrive to drop Rob and Jim, a move that stifles the buzz.

When we loaded, I saw that Tom guided Norman into the van. I make an updated mental note on a previous one about securing a step stool for the whales and their high-altitude seats. Maybe Al could construct something.

While Tom visits the bank, Norman and I sit in the van where Norman begins to fidget and groan.

"You all right, Norman?"

"No, it's my legs, mainly my left one. I got a lot of

pain. I think I slept on it wrong, or something."

With another stop due before heading home, I'm facing a "situation."

Norman complains about Rob the Second, saying that he should not be assigned to respite because he's not a military veteran.

Where did Norman pick up that notion? Without belaboring the point, I observe that a man does not have to be a veteran, although sometimes it seems that way because VA has a special arrangement for veterans through a homelessness project grant. Also, I conjecture that one reason for veterans' overrepresentation might relate to their enjoying more direct access to medical care than the general homeless population.

Norman is silent.

Tom is back in an Albuquerque minute and we go to Walmart with the conversation turning to phone cards and cell phones. My riders are amused when I comment that I avoid carrying mine so that my wife cannot contact me to run errands.

After Tom leaves us, Norman and I are parked about a hundred feet from the "Market" door at Walmart where his condition worsens. He moans more audibly. I ask about pain medicine.

"I took two Vicodin this morning but they aren't working. Maybe I need to take another one."

My reflex reaction is to second that idea. But I have sworn to avoid practicing law without a license and now I apply the same oath to medicine.

"We better have Jennifer call someone when we get back, Norman."

He accepts that and encourages Tom, at an unhearable distance in the store, to "hurry up."

To expedite matters, I move to a parking slot nearer the door and scurry inside. Tom stands at the fast food counter where he promised to pick up a soda for Norman. "I got so hungry waiting in line that I ordered something for myself."

We hustle back to the whale, and I challenge posted speed limits in hauling us back to the center where Norman cannot engineer his way out of the front seat. Tom lines up to help but he has his own problems, with cancer. So I wrap my arms around Norman and guide him to the concrete. He stands but does not move. "I don't think I can walk with this leg."

I advise Norman and Tom to wait outside while complimenting the weather god or goddess for a change in the weather, bringing a 50-degree, calm winter day. Inside, I seek out Jennifer and tell her about Norman. She mentions a problem with Norman's legs related to severe eczema. "The doctor said it's the worst case he has seen. The problem is that if Norman itches too much and opens up the sores, infection can set in." I also learn that Norman has a thyroid problem on top of everything.

I stride to the back storeroom where I have seen a walker. Al helps me locate it, lurking between two bicycles. A wheelchair sits next to the walker.

Back vanside, I maneuver Norman into the walker but he stops after taking an uncertain step.

I should have brought the wheelchair. "Do you think you'd do better with the wheelchair?"

"Yeah, I think so."

Now I trot to the back to retrieve the walker's neighbor. Then with Jennifer and Tom steadying Norman from the front, I guide the chair beneath him and he plops down. "This feels better," Norman says. I wheel him into respite and place his soda on the dining table, asking if he wants to lie down.

"No, I'll try it here." Without warning he breaks down, sobbing. "I don't want to be like this."

No one does. But how can I express any comeback without being misunderstood? I am like the counselor confronted by some grieving soul who asks, "Why me?" Honesty compels the response, "Why not you?" Random plays no favorites. Some people see nobility or opportunities for moral growth when confronted with debilitating illness. Bully for them. I see inexplicable suffering.

Jennifer offers reassurances to Norman, and I volunteer to take him to emergency if needed. She puts in a call to Norman's case worker, and to fill time I visit the storeroom to undertake the Sisyphusian task of organizing clothing. The donations are overflowing the sorting tables. To personify the mess, I imagine individual clothing items breeding, a la rabbits, when none of us is watching.

Checking back outside, I find that Jennifer has made contact with the medical people and will take Norman to an emergency room.

I nudge Norman up into the van and Jennifer drives off. What will his diagnosis will be? If it's an infection or blood clot, I'm going to call a come-to-Jesus meeting with Random or a member of Random's entourage. Enough is enough.

My empathy app kicks in as I remember that Norman is ten years younger than I. He suffers these multiple maladies while I take no prescription medicines and dare to complain about a recalcitrant plantar wart and touchy lower back. Get a life, Fred. Or, better yet, become more appreciative of the one you have.

Chapter FIFTEEN

A new year has dawned, although Norman's leg problem belongs to the old one. He updates me as he, Jim, and I chug along to the Cancer Center in the welcome prodigal, the Gray Ghost.

"Oh, it's fine now," Norman says about his leg. "I think it was just what I said it was. I slept on it wrong and it acted up."

Norman's recovery meshes with a chance encounter on New Year's Eve, promising another year of adventures and revelations at the Albuquerque Opportunity Center. I reckon that I have yet to see everything, despite brushes with several honorable mentions.

To celebrate New Year's Eve, my wife and I were waiting for a table at a popular steak restaurant. We planned to eat and run, heading home where at 10 p.m., Mountain Time, we would repeat our recent-years' ritual of slumping into overstuffed chairs facing our living room TV to watch the ball drop at Times Square, then hie off to bed. Whoopee.

After twenty minutes in the restaurant's bar area, we were still on hold when he walked in—he being Rob the Second, an age-appropriate woman clinging to his arm.

I spotted him first. After giving my wife a condensed bio, I tapped Rob on the shoulder as he signed up on the wait list. I played it straight. "Hey, Rob. How you doing?"

He turned and responded in kind, guileless. "Oh, Fred. Good to see you, man."

We introduced ourselves all the way around while I asked myself how often Rob left respite at night, and why he should take up space there if he could mange to be out and about in style. Besides, going AWOL from the Albuquerque Opportunity Center is prohibited.

We had not gone beyond small talk when our table for two came up, and all present exchanged a round of "Happy New Year." As my wife and I sat, she marveled that a respite resident would be sampling Albuquerque night life.

"It is a bit unusual," I understated. "It's not supposed to happen, but it does. Anyway, from all appearances Rob will have a place to sleep tonight." Then, weighing up conflicting obligations to the center and to Rob, I elected to keep our meeting to myself. Staying out overnight is a major no-no, but I'll let the staff enforce sanctions when they find them.

Now, I have dropped Norman at the Cancer Center for scheduled radiation, and Jim and I gossip about Norman on the way to the VA. "Good-hearted" is a characterization we agree on, although Jim amplifies on that.

"Oh, yeah, he's good-hearted, all right. But he can drive you crazy sometimes. Like today when the health-care people came, I was talking with one of them and he came over and started dominating the conversation. He dominates lots of conversations."

Although Jim's CAT scan for monitoring his aneurism is set for the tail end of January, he seeks an earlier appointment. "The problem seems to be getting worse. I don't feel so hot. I'm worried." Outside the hospital entrance, Jim tells me to go on, foreseeing complications in lobbying for the new date.

Back to fetch Norman, I sit in the cancer center's waiting room. I interrupt reading a dated magazine to observe Norman's fellow patients come and go. Some wear hats or caps to cover hair loss. Some appear hale and hearty, although others define cadaverous. Playing a quirky personification game, I theorize that if cancer were a human being it would be Adolf Hitler. Alzheimer's or any form of dementia would be Joe Stalin.

Norman finishes his treatment, chatting up his attendant nurse as he takes leave. He has managed to undergo more than half his quota, a fact he repeats to the appointment scheduler behind the front desk before announcing the magic number to one and all within earshot. Bless him.

Instead of returning to the center or even stopping by Mickey D's, we anticipate two meaningful stops—one at the state security office to apply for Food Stamps and another at the inevitable Walmart to cash a money-gram.

It's been months since I accompanied anyone to the state office, but the impression sticks of a teeming waiting area. With the trip to a box store on our agenda, an overtime morning looms. I don't mind. Before Norman's arrival, I might have minded, but I am learning about tolerance—among other things—from Norman.

"They said it would only take ten minutes," Norman says of his projected Food Stamp interview.

His optimism is admirable but not contagious. "Norman, I've been there and done that with other respite men, and I never knew anybody to get out of there in less than an hour. It's not so much the interview with the staff that's the problem, but the waiting. You sign in and then wait and wait and wait some more until you're called."

"Well, they told me ten minutes."

Why extend this conversation? Literally, time will tell.

Norman enters the building while I take up the hunt for a parking spot. The lot is packed, and I claim a place only because someone pulls out. This is not a good omen. I reach Norman as he signs in amid a constant hum from overlapping conversations in the standing-room "holding pen." The receptionist wears a security guard uniform and asks Norman to empty his pockets into a plastic container. He accomplishes this while I inquire about the wait time. She estimates two hours.

Norman reacts first. "Holy shit. Two hours?" He begins to scoop up his change and other pocket contents. "I'll come back tomorrow. What time do you open?"

"At eight. But try to get here by seven-thirty. You can wait in line outside until eight, and if you're in the first five you can get right in."

This prospect harkens to die-hard sports fans who camp outside stadiums to buy crow's nest tickets to the big game.

Norman frowns, and I thank the guard-greeter who proved to be attentive despite the hubbub engulfing her. On the way to the van, Norman fumes about the snag in applying for food stamps, although he acknowledges that he had better do so soon. He faces a one-week deadline.

We explore options for tomorrow. Maybe Jennifer could bring him at seven-thirty and I could pick him up for radiation. That seems far-fetched as I picture a shivering Norman stuck in line, although those around him would not lack for conversation—one-sided.

We press on to Walmart for the money-gram. "A woman up in Colorado sent me one," Norman says, offering no further information.

He stays inside the superstore beyond our expectations. After close to half an hour, he appears. I don't need to hear an explanation for the delay, but he provides one. "The reason it took so long was that I had to fill out another form."

Filling out extra forms has become, to borrow the Latin, *pro-forma*, and I think about the threatened second round of finger-printing and document update for the Veterans Affairs. What happened to that nuisance? Don't ask, and maybe no one will tell.

***

Time passing is a great problem-solver. Within days after seeing Rob the Second out on the town, I learn that he has been shifted to the general population, so our little secret becomes irrelevant to respite space.

"It's a done deal," Jennifer says. "We moved him this morning. He's more than ready to be over there. You know, when I moved his things an empty prescription bottle of oxycodone fell out of his duffel bag. I wonder if he's hooked on that stuff."

I wish otherwise. I would like to think that Rob requires a little—or big—something extra for his post-op pain and breathing hitches.

My constant companions these days, Norman and Jim, are with me. During our drive to radiation, I ask Norman about the Food Stamp application process and learn that it went without a hitch on my day off, despite the predicted wait.

"Oh, yeah, I got out of there in an hour and a half and my card was waiting for me the next day," Norman says. "I get $200 a month."

I translate this into more Walmart visits.

"And, you know, they roll that over. So, if I only spend $100 one month, I have $300 credit the next month."

Jim was less fortunate. "I couldn't get Food Stamps in Texas. My official residence is over there, but when I applied they found out that I'd been charging stuff and living over here for a few weeks, and they turned me down. And Texas doesn't allow rollovers. I found that out."

And I am finding out more and more about the vagaries of social service networks state by state.

After dropping Norman, I follow Jim's directions to a pawn shop north of downtown where he intends to reclaim a watch. I ask Jim about Henry's. He knows of it but says that pawn shop has closed down, leading me to speculate over the whereabouts of that colorful couple running the place when I visited there with Curtis. I hope they can afford retirement.

Jim apologizes for his transaction. "I haven't pawned anything since I was in my 20s. It's not a good deal but I needed some quick cash."

He goes inside the pawn shop but returns to ask whether I have eighteen dollars. I count my money and come up short. I never carry much cash, and fantasize that I could be featured in one of those old magazine ads by celebrities, asserting that they never carried more than fifty dollars with them. How many stick-ups did that prevent?

Jim apologizes once more. "They need that eighteen dollars for the interest. Sorry about that. But I've got a cash card. Do you know where there's an ATM around?"

No, but we will search. A convenience store across the way lives up to its name and Jim secures his cash. Within ten minutes, he retrieves the watch.

Jim also needs clothes washed and we pull into a coin laundry. He hauls his belongings inside and is back in minutes, smiling. "There's a woman in there who will do the washing and drying and folding, all for six dollars. That's a deal. It only costs a few bucks extra."

I make a miscalculation by figuring that we are set to pick up Norman.

"Fred, if you don't mind, I need to go to another pawn shop to pick up something else. Would it be possible for you to come back here in an hour and pick up my laundry? I won't need a ride back from the pawn shop."

That's a decent trade-off. "Sure, I can do that." And will.

Norman has been waiting an inordinate time to be picked up. No sooner have I parked half a football field away from the hospital door than he is making his way toward me. I apologize.

"Oh, don't worry none about it," Norman says. "I need the exercise."

I take Norman with me to the coin laundry to gather Jim's belongings, and by mid-morning we are back at the center where I bid Norman goodbye and place Jim's folded clothes on his bed, his shirts on hangers no less. Time allows for taking four bundles of discarded clothing to Goodwill and drop off surplus books from our library at the Barrett House outlet.

The clothes delivery presents extra work this time around because some genius has broken into the discarded clothing bags and rummaged through them. Never mind that the better goods already are visible to all on our clothing racks. In fact, at the moment the metal rods are groaning with pants, and shirts, and even suits, while the bins are stuffed with socks and underwear. No, never mind that. All evidence to the contrary, some descendant of Sherlock Holmes has deduced that a conspiracy is afoot at the Albuquerque Opportunity Center, namely that we are cheating him—and it is a he—by negotiating under-the-table deals with Goodwill and the like to slip them the good stuff. Sigh.

I long for a return of the efficient twenty-something woman who came to us months ago to perform community service. What she had done to invoke a court order, I never knew. But I do know that she was a champion clothes-sorter. With an assist from my fellow volunteer Howard, she had the clothing area in tip-top shape during her time. T-shirts in particular stood out, folded and stacked by size. Ah, those were the days.

Al helps out with my redundant chore by providing heavy-gauge plastic bags to repack the discarded clothes, which have accumulated in Howard's absence. He has traveled back East after his brother's death. I heave the four bags into the Ghost along with a box of books and set forth.

The Ghost's gas gauge reads a scosh below an eighth of a tank. That's a relief because I can avoid taking it for a refill, feeling no guilt about not reporting the gasoline level. An eighth of a tank does not satisfy my definition of low.

***

Norman has reached single digits in his radiation treatments. "Only eight more after today," he says on the way to the Cancer Center. "I'll be out of here the first week of next month."

I ask where he will end up.

"I'm all set up at the veterans' home down in Truth or Consequences."

"I've heard of it. I remember two guys from respite who went down there." I neglect to add that one was so bored by the isolation that he high-tailed it back to Albuquerque.

Norman recites a chapter of state history. "Yeah, T or C. Lots of people who don't know beans about New Mexico don't believe there is such a place. But there is. It was named after Ralph Edwards' radio show way back. Did you know that?"

Now I can play one-up. "Yes, I did. Believe it or not, Norman, I listened to that show on Saturday nights with my parents when I was a boy, and I remember when Ralph Edwards dared a town to change its name to Truth or Consequences. I believe the original name of the place was Hot Springs."

"Man, you're old, Fred. Anyhow, when I get down there they'll bring me back up to Albuquerque to the VA hospital for checkups. That way, I won't have to come back to UNM no more, except maybe for a skin graft."

Score another point for the good old Veterans Affairs.

After Norman wraps up his treatment, he performs his routine, announcing to the assemblage that he has "only" eight treatments left. Smiles greet this news. Norman has gained mascot status here.

Norman possesses a twenty-five-dollar gift certificate for a local supermarket chain and is eager to buy pills to combat itching. As he analyzes it, "That radiation travels around and dries up my skin all over the place, not just my back."

After my predictable false start, necessitating that special forbidden turn, we locate the right store, pull into a half-full parking lot, go in, and select the house brand of Benadryl. We make our way toward a checkout lane. Now, we can pay up and go back to the center. Well, almost.

"I need me some cigarettes before we go," Norman says.

Again, if cigarettes were illegal drugs, I would be subject to a charge of contributing to the delinquency of a senior—multiple counts.

No doubt sensing complications after sizing us up, a red-bloused employee beckons us from the back of a line and helps locate generic cigarettes for less than five dollars a pack. Norman picks up four. A rough calculation indicates that the whole shebang should amount to right at twenty-five dollars, including tax. Our minder rings up the sale. The grand total works out to twenty-six even. Norman fumbles for the extra money, but I see no bills sticking out of his wallet. "Here," I say, forking over a single.

"Thanks, Fred, I owe you that dollar."

"Don't worry about it. You had a birthday not too long ago. Consider it a late gift."

"Okay, but tell you what I'll do. Come down to T or C to see me and I'll take you out to K-Bob's for one of their steak dinners. They've got all kinds of steaks."

"I bet they have chicken-fried steaks. My family thinks that's funny, but I like those, really."

"Oh, come on, Fred. We can do better than that. I'll buy you a real steak."

"Norman, that's a deal."

Chapter SIXTEEN

There's trouble in paradise. A shaggy-haired man, distinguished by a blank gaze reminiscent of the one thousand-yard stare attributed to some combat veterans, has upset the routine. He transmits that chilling, see-through look my way as I descend the respite stairs to collect Jim and Norman. Inside the van, they report that the new visitor gobbled up someone else's breakfast despite being warned not to.

"He's not all there, one taco short of a combo plate," is Norman's diagnosis. Norman is not implying, however, that he would forgive the new bunk mate for helping himself to Norman's stash of food and drink in the respite fridge. "If I find him getting in my stuff, he'll be in big trouble. I'm serious. I'm not putting up with that from nobody, crazy or not."

Jim adds that the man was lurking around his bunk. "I was pretending to be asleep. He didn't take anything, but it's only a matter of time. Next thing, he'll be stealing more than food. A guy who'll steal food will steal more valuable stuff. Believe me, I know the type."

I believe him.

After a routine ride to the Cancer Center, Jim and I wait for Norman to finish radiation. Afterward, Norman relates a success during today's treatment. "They rubbed that place there on my back, not hard, and you should have seen all the dead skin that fell off. That's a good sign, and it didn't hurt one bit."

Talk turns to Social Security disability because Norman is awaiting word from his advocate attorney in Colorado. Why Colorado? "Somebody referred me there. I guess I could have used somebody more local, but it's too late now." I remember a reference to a Colorado woman who forwarded a money-gram to Norman and figure that the money represented an advance to be deducted from Norman's payout.

Norman has a secondary interest in Social Security, his son's predicament in Roswell. "I don't know, I have to wonder about him. He's got some problems, but he's got a job in a sheltered workshop deal. Of course, he went and lost his Social Security. I told him he had to report his income to the ISD or he'd lose out."

"ISD?" I continue to suffer from acronym overload.

"Income Support Division at the state. See, he was making more than $2,000 but he didn't report it like he should have. I told him. But would he listen? So now he lost out. Of course, these women who drop one baby after another, they can go and get their Social Security anytime they want."

I cannot verify and will not inquire about how Norman is privy to this information. I execute a right-angle turn in the conversation and ask Jim about his destination.

Jim says he needs to visit a motel office on Central Avenue at the east edge of Albuquerque. He has word that the place offers veterans housing discounts, and he intends to sign up. We find the location after some fits and starts because due to an oversight we did not have the address or even the cross street. I had to slow to a creep as we scanned storefronts. In a couple of instances my pace proved too pokey even for those in the slow lane, who swished around me in what I would call churlish fashion. Why can't other drivers follow my spotless example and exhibit saint-like patience and exemplary driving habits on our roadways? Ahem. Regardless, we have too many drivers going slow in the fast lane and fast in the slow lane to suit me and, I dare say, other pilgrims on our roadways.

Jim is in and out of the place almost as soon as I let him off and back the Ghost into a parking space. He reports that he has signed up for a two-man room. "I don't like the idea of roommates. It's pretty much the luck of the draw, but that's the way it is here," he says.

On our return leg to home base, via Walmart, Jim opens up. "I may not look like much now, but I was in construction for sixty-five years and had a successful career."

My elementary subtraction generates a personal question. "How old are you, Jim?"

"I'm seventy-nine and started laying cement blocks when I was fourteen."

I'm in awe. The math adds up, underlining my miscalculation about Jim's age. I would have judged him to be a decade younger with a trim white beard that could have been painted on his face. He wears a classic black Stetson and looks more like a retired college professor than I do. My nosy self wants to know how articulate and knowledgeable Jim landed at the Albuquerque Opportunity Center, although I will not pry today. These matters often bubble to the surface in their own time.

At the store, Norman leaves us while Jim and I tour the parking aisles for a prime spot. Bored, Jim asks to get out. "I guess I'll go in there, too. I promise not to get lost."

Norman and Jim emerge with a basketful of groceries contained in a sea of half-full plastic bags. Norman comments. "They give me lots of bags so that no one gets too heavy. I can't lift much with my arms the way they are."

I look over the contents. "I see you have lots of frozen dinners there, Norman."

"I get tired of the stuff they give us. It gets old after a while." And Norman has been with us for a while.

After helping my passengers unload the bags into respite, I give Jennifer a rundown on the morning, reporting that both men expressed disgust at the hirsute man's attitude and actions.

"We're on top of it," she says. "He was walking around without his pants yesterday, and I got him straightened out about that. And the food problem, too."

"Mental?" I ask this, although I already have two witnesses and my own eyes as confirmation.

"For sure. We're trying to find another place for him. But it's a hard go when they have mental problems. He was here for a week before and just disappeared one night."

I also talk about Jim's application for housing at the veterans' discount motel.

I am treated to Jennifer's sly smile. "I know about that, too. He's been working on getting out of here ever since I told him he had to go over into the general population. When he first came, we said we'd give him five days in respite. It's going on thirty-five now. Incidentally, this is why he wants to move his medical appointment up. What a coincidence."

Yes, a coincidence.

***

Thanks to Norman I am eating crow—a dish that often stimulates my taste buds. Norman's final radiation appointment has arrived, and his ever-bright outlook has become infectious.

As he emerges from his last session, he recites a chronology of his treatments and prospects at the veterans' home to me and the appointment woman behind the desk. He is due back at the hospital in six weeks to gauge prospects for a skin graft. "Doctor Campbell says he doesn't want to do a graft right away, in case the cancer comes back." From his breezy manner, Norman could be talking about a delayed hiatal hernia operation.

Norman's character shines through when he mentions his nurse. "Poor little Joan. Oh, I felt so sorry for her. She had tears in her eyes when we said goodbye. She told me, 'Norman, you've been a wonderful patient. We'll miss you.'"

Now for the serving of said delicacy. Norman's words evoke a few of mine, and they sting. I well remember opining that I saw no nobility or moral growth in the plight of the afflicted. Moral growth I'll leave to higher authority. But thanks to Norman, I have witnessed nobility in his face-off with death as he demonstrated optimism, bravery, and a consistent concern for others throughout. I'm not at all convinced that I will exhibit the same qualities when some god-awful malady strikes me.

He praises Jennifer. "She's really a fine person, you know. She is trying to get permission to take me down to T or C on Monday. I hope she can."

Meantime, we have a final stop at the Veterans Affairs hospital and Norman reminisces during our drive. "When I came up to Albuquerque back last fall, the doctors didn't give me much of a chance. One of them said, 'Norman, I don't know how you've made it this far.'" Norman flashes a victory smile and points an index finger upward. "I said, 'I know how I made it this far. The good Lord was looking after me. He and Jesus Christ have a plan for me and it's working.'"

I throttle the impulse to ask why the good Lord couldn't have done a better job of looking after Norman in the first place, thereby negating his pain and suffering. But I am not going down that road with Norman— or anyone else.

Norman promises to be back in touch with all of us at the center when he attains a clean bill of health. "You know what I'd like to do? I'd like to come back to the AOC and volunteer, maybe drive respite men around. I'd like that."

"Norman," I say, "you can have my job." What possesses me in these moments?

Norman remonstrates. "Oh, no, Fred, I wouldn't do that. I wouldn't want to take anyone's job away. Oh, no."

"Just kidding, Norman."

"Oh, I thought so."

I steer into the VA drop-off. We have reached the end of the ride and the end of our association, for now. Someone else will collect Norman here later.

I tend to collapse into an "aw shucks" mannerisms when saying goodbyes. Norman shows me the way.

"Thanks, Fred. You and all the others have been real decent to me and I appreciate it. I guess we won't see each other before I leave."

"No, but let's count on connecting when you come up here for an appointment."

"Let's make it happen," Norman says, sliding out of his seat. As he turns his back to walk toward the sliding glass doors, I stare at the letters "NAM" stitched onto the back strap of his cap.

You know, New Mexico is a fine place to live, but the desert plants spew waves of pollen, leading to allergy reactions almost non-stop. Right now, for instance, I'm reaching for my handkerchief. Something must be in the air.

Chapter SEVENTEEN

Norman is not the only absentee from respite today. The unkempt-hair-and-beard man is missing—departed under his own steam.

"He up and walked away the other night, the same way he did before," Jennifer says. "Poor guy."

I take an amateur's sashay into philosophy. "I guess it's a utilitarian kind of situation, the greatest good for the greatest number and all that. If he'd stayed around he would have caused headaches for everybody. I think he already did."

Jennifer agrees but adds, "I suppose. But I always wonder what happens to those guys who are mentally off balance. Where do they sleep? Who feeds them? What do they do all day?"

Good questions. But for now I need to home in on collecting a new charge. Down in respite, I find a stocky fellow with dark hair, thinning on top but offset by a lush full beard. Apologetically, he asks if a visit to a coin laundry would be possible.

"Sure, I can do that." I could have added, "and have done so many times."

Those times may be ending. A move is afoot to install a laundry as part of an AOC expansion.

Although costly, the expense of setting up our own laundry will pale in comparison with the long-term bill for sheets and pillow cases and towels, picked up, washed, and returned by A-1 Linen Supply. For a reason unremembered, I once saw a four-month laundry bill for the center. It surpassed five thousand dollars for a total weight approaching ten thousand pounds. Yes, the on-site laundry cannot come soon enough, although "soon" implies a flexible timetable.

In the form of a question, I suggest to my new acquaintance that we make for the closest self-serve laundry. "The one on Fourth next to Walgreen's?"

He is agreeable.

After he frees himself from medical students performing their once-a-week visit to monitor for vital signs, set up appointments, and tend to overall medical concerns for respite men, the new man and I meet up in the Gray Ghost. I introduce myself, and he answers with his name, Hank, and a firm handshake. He speaks clearly and distinctly with a sophisticated air that supports another stereotype: At one time Hank performed indoor work with no heavy lifting. Without prompting, he tells his story.

He once taught at a local high school and later worked in a business office. (Aha, for once a stereotype is confirmed.) "My job went to India and then I went to Arizona where I also was laid off." Back here and looking for work, he made an ill-fated decision to attend the annual Fourth of July fireworks show at Albuquerque's Balloon Fiesta Park.

Hank fills me in on a fire that broke out there. "The media got that wrong, by the way. They said that the fireworks set off the fire, but it was the fire that came in and set off the fireworks. It was wild." He gestures, using the forefinger of his right hand to trace an elliptical path above his head.

"I'd sold a diamond stick pin for seven hundred dollars and didn't want to walk around with that kind of money. So I left most of it in my glove box when I parked for the fireworks. When the fire came, there was no way to get to my car because the firefighters and police had the way blocked. So a friend and I took a bus back and then I got dropped at my motel. The next morning they took me back to the lot and the car was gone. I assumed it was towed, but the police had no record of it. Sure enough, it was stolen. My world turned upside down then, and I was on the streets for a long time before I found out about this place."

Frostbite bit him during his street life. On one of the year's coldest nights, he says he was jumped behind a car wash where he was sleeping out on East Central Avenue. "When I came to, my right shoe was missing and my sock was all wet and frozen. At first, pink-colored flesh flaked off my toes, but now they're turning darker because of bad circulation. I'm worried."

I would be, too. I learn that he has an appointment tomorrow at Health Care for the Homeless. I promise to take him.

Hank has related a twice-told tale, or I should say an oft-told tale. I presume that a number of these accounts are spun out to the point of no return, but the law of averages says that others must be true. I place a cyber bet on Hank's being fact-based.

When I drop Hank, I hold out hope that I will be available to collect him later. He estimates a little more than an hour for washing and drying. I tell him to call if he can, and he gives me his cell number. Hank's having a cell phone is not unusual. Those devilish mixed breeds of convenience and annoyance often find their way into the hands of my men.

Back at the center I catch up with fellow volunteer Howard, as he is sorting clothes. The disarray on the table represents a reminder of many a visit to the back room. We lament the fact that gremlins seem to inhabit the space at night, creating all manner of mischief. Howard suggests installing surveillance cameras. Smiling, he points toward the ceiling.

I dismiss that idea. "Have you seen the costs of those things? It might be cheaper for the center to pay you and me to stake out this area in night shifts."

"Yes, why don't you suggest that, Fred?" Howard interprets my offering in the way in which it was intended—nonsensical.

Jennifer arrives and commiserates. "Sorry about the mess. It was probably men trying on clothes."

With a cocked eyebrow I stare at Jennifer inquiring whether someone in authority could fire off a memo directing staff to assure that "shoppers" return clothing rejects to the racks. She pledges to do it, and leaves us.

Howard changes the subject. "Remember when we picked up those snazzy suits and sport coats donated by that men's store?"

Certainly. I helped with that loading project and worked up a sweat as we stacked piles of clothing inside the wheelchair van. Howard says the store's apparent generosity amounts to no more than a public relations ploy and tax write-off, but I regard the store's gesture as including a grain of philanthropy.

Howard was around when the suits were modeled. "You should have seen it, Fred. It was like Christmas. The guys would take turns admiring each other dressed up fit to kill." The suit supply certainly has dwindled.

More than an hour goes by, and I remember to call Hank. I make my way through the main dorm to reach the front office and pick up the desk phone. Per usual, my cell phone rests at home. The desk phone line is dead. Jennifer comes by and repeating my effort, dials 9 with no result. She raises the telephone console off the desk, and we find that the consarned thing has been disconnected. I pick up the cord with the jack end lying on the floor. After a plug-in, the phone operates perfectly. I reach Hank, who complains that he has been calling but gets cut off after the first ring. Gee, how could that happen? Also, and more to the point, who accomplished this bothersome feat? It almost had to be staff. Jennifer says she will investigate.

On the way out to fetch Hank, I see Brian and ask about phone calls. He allows that it was strange that no incoming calls interrupted him this morning. Maybe someone on staff didn't want to be interrupted last night. And it occurs to me that the perpetrator of the phone disconnect could have played some part in the unwelcome clothing reorganization in the back. Quite a busy beaver last night, if so.

I pick up Hank, waiting curbside at the Laundromat, along with another new respite resident, Butch, who has made his way to the laundry by other means and appreciates the ride back. I explain about the phones, and Hank lets me know that he tried to reach us both from his cell and a public phone outside the coin laundry. Without putting my mind in gear, I engage my mouth and say that the telephone problem may well have been caused by staff. This sits well with my two riders. I try for a mid-course correction. "Of course nobody knows. It could have been anybody." I quit conjecturing while

I'm not too far in arrears, knowing that it could not have been "anybody." Not that many people have access to the front desk.

***

Reuben, a Native American, is riding with me to the First Nations social services office in Southeast Albuquerque. In a soft voice that verges on incoherence, he has spoken his name but otherwise remains silent as we glide along.

I have been told that Rueben suffered a knee injury when hit by a car. He joins that long list of those afflicted with leg problems after such run-ins. The standard scenario involves stepping off a curb in the middle of a dimly-lit block at night. Some men have filled in the blanks by admitting that they were drinking beforehand. Others have left those blanks empty.

Half way to our destination, Rueben asks, "Are you an Indiana fan?"

His question surprises me twice over. First, I had not expected him to begin a conversation. Second, I had forgotten which baseball cap I had chosen to complement my outfit today. Calling upon my keen deductive powers, I realize that I am wearing the red one with the white "IU" letters on front. Yes, I remember now and explain to Reuben about my master's degree from Indiana University.

Reuben comes up with an offbeat reason for asking about Indiana. "Did you know Bobby Knight?"

His interest in the famous, or infamous, basketball coach tickles me. "Well, not personally, but everybody in Indiana and about everywhere else in the United States knows about Bobby Knight."

It is Reuben who is amused now. "That guy really is a character." He gives out a guffaw.

"To say the least." And I reflect that in recent times my home state has been known to two of my riders for Ku Klux Klan activity and Bobby Knight. I would prefer the Indianapolis 500 and U.S. Sen. Richard Lugar.

Eager to know more about Reuben, besides wanting to change topics, I ask a standard question. "You have Social Security?"

"Heck, yeah—well almost. I can get it thanks to Jennifer helping me out. But now I have to find my sister. She has all my stuff and I can't find out where she is."

"Is there any other way for you to get help?"

"I could go back to the reservation, but it's too quiet there. I don't like it."

"Which reservation?"

"Crownpoint."

My spotty background knowledge of our native people marks Reuben as a Navajo.

We arrive at First Nations where Reuben is required to sign in and wait his turn in the inevitably crowded waiting room. Wherever and whenever I go, public agency facilities are chock-full of people, sometimes standing-room-only. I wish that one time I could enter an empty waiting room.

A woman on the sunny side of middle age and carrying a clipboard calls Reuben's name and he signals his presence. She asks what he needs. I assume it is the bum knee, bashed by the hit-and-run vehicle. But he reports that the knee injury is treated at Presbyterian Hospital. As he says this, I detect that his conversation is becoming more disjointed. Reuben repeats to the receptionist his concern about his sister and her where-abouts. He also brings up his plans for qualifying for Social Security disability.

The woman asks if his "vitals" have been checked.

Reuben maintains a blank stare.

After an appropriate wait, the woman says she will write in "vitals check" on his sheet.

I inquire about how long Reuben might be waiting. The woman leaves, returning to say that the process will take "quite a while."

Pointing out the phone number, I hand an AOC business card to Reuben and tell him to call for a ride, if needed. He nods, although he says he might hop on a bus. As I say goodbye, Reuben pumps my hand, and although we are well into February he wishes me a Happy New Year. I return the sentiment and say that I may see him the next day.

***

Injuries from falls, especially those linked to res-pite men's emerging as runners-up in tangles with motor vehicles, seem to be all the rage. Butch, the man I met last week with Hank, has a bandaged gash on his fore-head, plus a chronic bad knee from being hit by a car. In addition, Jennifer tells me, he has been diagnosed with cancer.

"He's in denial about that," Jennifer says. "He doesn't want to deal with it."

The knee is an old wound, but the gash came yesterday when he undertook a walk home from Univer-sity Hospital. Suffering balance problems, he fell some-where along the more than two-mile route. He made it back on his own, though, bloodied but unbowed.

I am scheduled to drive Butch for another hospital appointment and ask him about his ailments. "I hear that besides the cut and knee problem, you've got cancer. That seems like a bit of bad-luck overkill."

"Seems like it. I don't like to talk about the cancer too much. It's breast cancer."

That explains some things. But from reading, plus one personal contact, I am aware that breast cancer is not unknown among men, and I say so.

My understanding is appreciated. "You're a good fellow for knowing that. A lot of people I run into think I'm putting them on about it. But it's real."

When we approach the hospital drop-off, Butch asks to be let out at the smoking "pen," the designated area bordering the overhang. I watch him join a knot of smokers where one gives Butch a high sign. Do the smoking companions know about Butch's form of cancer?

Chapter EIGHTEEN

> *Spring*
> *Has sprung*
> *The grass has riz*
> *Where last year's*
> *Careless drivers is*

Not for the first time, I am astounded, astonished, amazed or dismayed—whichever modifier packs the most punch—by what I remember and what I don't. The other day, I went charging into a room at home where I forgot what mission propelled me there. Bill Cosby does a routine on that, talking about the eyes trying to help by casting about in all directions. But my latest episode involves long-term memory. The doggerel above harks to boyhood days and roadside Burma Shave signs. It is said that the Interstate system killed off those shaving-cream gems when readability suffered from widened rights-of-way and increased highway speeds. American civilization lost something there.

The point of this remembrance of stuff past is that spring has sprung with the coming of May, and with May comes the annual "Sleep Out" fund-raiser sponsored by the city's homlelessness project. I am tempted to ask the staff why the organization doesn't sponsor a "Sleep In," but I have pledged to curb my impertinent impulses and become more charming.

The Sleep Out echoes those "walkathons" for various charities. In our case, the staff solicits sponsorships for themselves and center residents to sleep under the stars or in a tent for a night. Our staff organizer, Amanda Clearwater, has generated a ton of publicity for the Sleep Out, scheduled on private school property. Said publicity promises "a movie, music, and fun." The "fun" I struggle to imagine. The goal is to raise awareness along with $25,000 through corporate help, $30 individual donations, and $50 family donations. Volunteers are being enlisted.

When approached by Amanda to take part in the "fun," however, I beg off. "Listen, Amanda, I earned a camping merit badge in Boy Scouts and ever since have patronized these modern establishments called motels. These conveniently located accommodations offer clean beds, bathrooms, and hot showers. Perhaps you've heard of them." (So much for my charm offensive.)

Receiving a well-earned sneer from Amanda and pestered by guilt, I volunteer to show up on an "off" day, Friday, to pitch in with set-up.

Amanda seems pacified. "That will be most welcome, Fred. Howard is supposed to come in and you two can run errands and then help get things organized over at the school."

***

Howard and his truck are waiting for me at the center at mid-morning. It's warm and sunny, and he has his half-ton, dented white pickup ready for action on Sleep Out night day.

Howard has our marching orders. "We're sup-

posed to pick up a barbeque grill at this woman's house
way out off West Central. She's a friend of Al's. Then
Amanda wants us to go to a couple of markets to collect
fruits and vegetables for the cookout."

I appreciate Howard and his positive take on life.
Last month he wrote in our newsletter about his role at
the Albuquerque Opportunity Center.

"I retired from the Air Force an officer.

*"I retired from the University of New Mexico a
director.*

*"Now I'm a janitor, driver and stock guy—and I
love it."*

Amen, Howard. I could not have said it better,
and thus won't try. I remember my own proclamation
on the day I retired: no more meetings and no more
potlucks. Full disclosure: The potluck pledge has been
revoked when the meal showed extraordinary promise.

Howard and I begin our scavenger hunt by
heading out for the grill. Howard has the address, and
with map in hand I try to direct him. We are winding
through a subdivision where the ranch-style houses on
average could stand upgrading. A fence is sagging here
and a yard is barren there. Not all the houses carry numbers, but through the process of elmination we pull up
to the best-guessed address.

We step along a cracked walkway and tap on
the front door. No one answers, and we express mutual
doubts that anyone is around. No cars are to be seen. All
is quiet. I do notice, however, a hefty grill sitting in the
side yard. I contemplate commandeering it. We knock
again with no response, but as we turn away and agree
to leave without our prize, a twentyish, T-shirted fellow
appears at the door.

He apologizes about not responding sooner, but says he has no information about the grill. "Maybe mom knows," he says, pulling out a cell phone. After a brief conversation, he smiles and nods before signing off. "Okay, she says you can take it."

When it comes to heavy-duty labor, neither Howard nor I are what we used to be. Probably, I never was. The cast-iron barbecue grill is a barrel type, complete with side shelving. It proves cumbersome. After Howard and I struggle with it, the young man gets involved and we manhandle the beast into the pickup bed. I grab the propane tank, which we had the presence of mind to detach, and set it back under the grill. That baby is not going anywhere. We thank our benefactor's son and are on our way.

The drive to the first food market takes fifteen minutes as Howard and I congratulate ourselves on putting the toughest chore behind us. We pull into the market, and hanging back I allow Howard to do the talking. We might as well have crash-landed from Mars.

"Sorry, but I don't know what you're talking about," says the manager after Howard explains our presence. "I don't know who the woman you mention talked with but it wasn't me. Sorry I can't help you."

At least the manager was polite about the communication breakdown. Nothing to do but leave. "Makes you wonder how we will fare at the next place," I say while we drive toward a Fourth Street location.

Second address, first address result. I'm beginning to question whether Amanda made those calls, or instead figured that produce managers would pity two geezers and hand over some wilted surplus commodities. Howard and I are eager to meet up with Amanda and cross examine her to get this matter cleared up, but neither of us has a cell phone. This is another way that Howard and I think alike.

Leaving the parking lot, we are greeted by a dip in the pavement as we pull onto bustling Fourth Street. I think I detect a thud coming from the truck bed.

"Did you hear anything, Howard?"

"I may have. I'm not sure."

"Pull around the corner and I'll check."

As soon as Howard rolls to a stop on a nearby side street, I hop out and survey the scene. Well, the gas tank is there but something is missing—namely, the grill. Howard has piled out of the driver's side, and I look at him, and he looks at me, and we look back toward the roadway, and then we look at each other again. If my face defines panic the same way as Howard's, the freeze-frame depicting our expressions would qualify for a classic portrait, something like that "Scream" painting.

Our grill and its various components are scattered in the middle of Fourth Street, and southbound vehicles are creeping along to dodge the debris field. In times such as these I regret not paying more attention to that graduate school lecture on crisis management. Incapacitated for a second or two, I can do no better than blurt out an obvious plan of action. "I'll run out there and start gathering the stuff up, Howard, if you'll pull the truck out into the turn lane so we can start loading." Sprinting toward the street, I send along a paen to some long-ago city planner who insisted on inserting a turn lane into this stretch of road.

I reach the middle lane and assess the damage. The grill's main body is intact, even though it must have made quite an impact on the asphalt after it toppled off the truck. However, shelving parts, along with two legs and two wheels, have detached themselves, along with odd-shaped parts I cannot identify. Howard's truck has reached the scene, and we start hauling metal into the turn lane. A driver honks his horn in passing. At golf tournaments he must be the idiot who hollers out, "In the hole!" when a ball is driven off a tee.

Then an angel appears. Where he came from I don't know and he doesn't say. I assume he came from a strip mall store across the street, but that is beside the point. The point is that he is assisting with the clean-up, commenting, "I saw what happened. I guess you all didn't have the grill tied down."

Right, although I could have survived until Doomsday without that observation. I appreciate the fellow, however, when he provides a necessary boost to situate the dinged-up barrell of the grill back onto the truck bed where we center it. After odds and ends are rounded up, Howard and I offer simultaneous words of appreciation to our angel before he darts back across the street.

I glare at the undeployed bungee cords lying serenely on the truck bed and pick them up. Without saying a word, Howard and I begin a series of figure-eight maneuvers, girdling the grill before securing the bungee's hook ends.

"Damn, Howard, I never thought that thing with all its weight would move, let alone tip over. It sure was top-heavy." Whether I am trying to console myself or Howard, I don't know. Relief and the absurdity of the scene provoke mutual snickers.

Funny how swiftly fickle fortune switches sides, spinning your life around on a dime. Minutes ago

Howard and I were all lathered up, keen to interrogate Amanda about the wild goose chases for fruits and vegetables. But at this juncture we are not relishing meeting up with her—ever. Maybe she'll be occupied at the home office when we deliver our battered cargo to the Sleep Out site.

No such luck. Amanda is on the scene, overseeing a tent-raising and the placing of one of those blow-up plastic columns that flutter outside stores sponsoring special events. On this windless day, it stands erect.

"How did it go, guys?" What a question.
Howard and I trade mournful glances. Because he provided the truck and fuel and then dealt with the produce people, I feel duty-bound to step forward. "Well, for starters neither of the managers at the fruit and vegetable stands knew anything about the Sleep Out. I guess you talked with people who weren't around today. I mean, they had no clue what we were asking about."

"Don't worry about it. We've got plenty of food. That was just for some extras. But you said 'for starters,' Fred. What else?"

"Uh, well, we had some trouble with the grill."

"You didn't get it?"

"Oh, yeah. We got it, all right."

"So, is there a problem?"

"Slightly." I can't draw this out, although I would love to. "For some reason that defies gravity the darn thing tipped off the back of the truck up on Fourth Street and has a dent or two. But the main body of it's intact. I'm pretty sure we can grill on it." (He said in a hopeful manner.)

God bless Amanda who appreciates the big picture. "Let's go take a look ."

We do, and determine that the legs, two wheels, and one side shelf can be reattached, more or less, to the main frame and make do. Amanda suggests that Howard and I take a lunch break and come back in the afternoon. Our hang-dog looks must have betrayed us.

***

I feel revived after a fast-food lunch and assume that Howard does, too. Our main job this afternoon involves setting up chairs and tables for the campers' supper. After we accomplish this without incident, we place paper covers on table tops. I am relieved to see that Amanda has enlisted two center residents to remove the damaged grill from Howard's truck and place it beside two undamaged ones for the cookout. I sense that Howard and I have closed out our heavy-lifting days, at least those required for this fundraiser.

A panel truck arrives carrying hamburger patties and hot dogs. A vendor has donated the whole lot, and his driver helps us offload the boxes of meat. He proves to be a cheery fellow, yet another happy warrior. The boxes are not heavy but they number in the dozens. As the work winds down, we come across containers of slaw and baked beans to be added to the mix. Another vehicle carrying bottled water and soft drinks arrives, and that lot is taken off and stacked behind the serving tables.

The grills are being fired up, signaling that my role in this affair is complete. Nobody but nobody has asked me to cook.

As the afternoon sun sags toward the horizon, a derelict pickup with a camper shell set into the bed cruises in. A man and a woman and a girl, whom I judge to be pre-double-digit years, pile out. The girl wears pig-tails and a winsome smile.

I overhear the couple's conversation with Aman-da. The man has lost his job in California, and they are on the road to Kansas where they have relatives. Images of Steinbeck's *Grapes of Wrath* family, the Joads, enter my mind, although these folks are dressed better and ap-pear to be on the favorable side of that demarcation be-tween down-and-out and hanging on by the fingernails. Also, they are migrating in the opposite direction than the Joads. The woman says they needed a place to stay in Albuquerque and were referred to the Sleep Out by a contact agency. They comment on their good fortune in being guests at the Sleep Out.

I appreciate the upbeat tone this trio brings to our event. The girl maintains her smile and asks Aman-da if she can visit a D J broadcasting from the grounds as part of the promotion. The girl is granted the go-ahead as long as she keeps quiet until the D J halts his patter and plays music.

Singling out Howard and Amanda, I say good-byes and walk toward my car, retrieved from the center on our way back from lunch. The family's camper-truck lies on the direct path to my car, and I am overcome by an urge to take an action that I cannot rationalize, now or ever. Passing along the side of the family's truck, I find a back window cracked open. I was hoping for such. Glancing around and not seeing anyone looking my way, I reach into one of my jeans' front pockets and pull out three greenbacks, constituting two Washing-tons and a Jackson. I peel off the twenty, crease it, and push it through the opening and onto a stack of clothes atop the back seat of the extended cab. I see a bare space on the far side, reserved no doubt for the girl.

If anyone would badger me about why I did what I just did, I would be struck dumb. I could not say. Guilt? Kneejerk behavior? Imagining the family's glee upon finding the twenty? Picturing my two daughters when they were young? Do gooderism? Honest charity? Who knows? And when you come right down to it, who cares? I suppose God, or whoever's running the universe these days, might shed some light on this business. But he, she, or it—as the case may turn out to be—isn't confiding in me. On second thought, maybe I did receive a celestial message that bypassed my radar a few moments ago.

Chapter NINETEEN

Jennifer is sitting at her desk, emitting an enigmatic smile accompanied by a cheery, "Oh, hi, Fred."

It's the week after the Sleep Out, and no doubt she is delighted by its success. "So, how did we come out on the fund-raiser, Jennifer? Make some money, did we?"

"Yes, thanks to Amanda, we did great. We hit our target and then some."

"Good for you. Twenty-five-thousand bucks will help the old budget. Congratulations." Having said that, I take a deep breath and broach the sensitive topic that I cannot sidestep. "How did all of the business with that woman's grill turn out?"

Jennifer retains her smile, even though she says, "Not so great. She pitched a fit, and we gave her two hundred and fifty dollars cash to get a new grill. She wanted more but we told her two-fifty was more than fair, considering the condition of her old one before .... well, before your incident. Also, she's mad at Al, who really had nothing to do with it. She won't talk to him and says she'll never have anything to do with him. Poor Al. His comment was, 'There goes my fry bread.' Evidently, she makes primo fry bread."

How considerate of Jennifer to talk about "your incident." I grapple for one more loose end. "I presume we kept the old grill. I mean, it was in working order despite the, uh, 'incident.'"

"No, Amanda had to give that back to her, too. The woman was impossible, and we wanted to get rid of her."

Now I, like the grill, am bent out of shape. I am not pleased one whit. By all rights, we should have kept the beat-up grill. "You know, Jennifer, two mistakes were made on that deal. The big one was when Howard and I didn't tie down the scruffy grill. But the little one was letting that sorry pirate make off with cash and the old one to boot. She's ripping us off. Geesh."

Jennifer shrugs. "Give it a rest, Fred. In the big picture it's not worth bothering about."

She's right. And I should be more than willing to let the subject drop, especially now that some impulse has motivated me to donate an extra hundred dollars to the homelessness project at Christmastime. But I can't understand Jennifer's continuing to smile, a knowing smile that was never so educated. Off balance, I await further conversation, which is not forthcoming so I forge ahead. "I sense you're trying to tell me something, Jennifer."

The smile continues to unnerve me. Given her disposition, I assume that her smile is one that says, "I know something about you that you don't know, and it's good news." This interpretation must be laid beside episodes from other occasions in my life when a rival smiled a smile that said, "I know something about you that you don't know, namely that you're about to get taken down by a Category 7 feces storm. Ha-ha." I always figured that as children those cretins peed in the sandbox when the other kids weren't looking.

"So what's up?"

"To cut to the chase, Fred, you've been named our volunteer of the year."

Shifting into false modesty gear—my favorite refuge—I come back with, "Me? Little ol' me, volunteer of the year?"

"That's right, seriously. What happens is that every agency connected with the Mayor's Office of Volunteerism and Engagement gets to nominate one of their volunteers for the award. There're about twenty-five programs involved all over the city. So you'll be honored down at City Hall at ten o'clock next Tuesday morning at a formal ceremony. Dennis and I will go with you."

"Let me check my calendar. Let's see we're into May so this can't be April First. No fooling allowed today. Now, let me review my schedule for next Tuesday." I close my eyes and count to five. "Okay, it appears that I can squeeze it in."

"You'd better. And cut the comedy. The staff chose you unanimously. You deserve it, so act like it."

"Yes, ma'am."

Heretofore, I've thought that these awards with their plaques and certificates bordered on—or slopped over into—the frivolous and redundant. What respectable person needs these pseudo-events to confirm his or her worth? Now that I will garner my own artifacts next week, however, my previous position is undergoing a major realignment. And it is comforting to realize that I was chosen from a volunteer pool of fourteen.

I go about my duties today with a renewed sense of mission for what I do here, not forgetting what this place does for me.

***

The reception room at City Hall is humming with the buzz of human voices, that universal tune accompanying formal or semi-formal events. The last time I heard this background occurred at a lavish wedding reception—not one I paid for. After identifying me as an award recipient, an aide ushers me into a front row seat and I say goodbye to my chaperones, Jennifer and Dennis. They approach a table topped by a punch bowl and cookies.

A woman to my left appears to be my junior, but when I query her about her years of volunteering, she replies, "Twenty-three." I'm thankful that she does not ask me the same question. Compared with twenty-three, my four years seem like a number more befitting a trainee. I fish for a different result on my right, and reel in a response of seventeen years. I decide to forgo further conversational icebreakers with fellow honorees.

The mayor's honcho for volunteer organizations calls the session to order and makes some remarks about "the need for citizens like you." Soon, she is calling the roll and more and more I feel like a piker. Most of my front-row companions have spent ten or more years with their agencies. About half way through the list, my name is read, followed by a rundown of my contributions to the Albuquerque Opportunity Center. Years of service are not mentioned. Jennifer and the staff have done more than right by me with their blurb. Also, I remind myself that our organization has been in business for a meager six years, putting me and us at a numerical disadvantage.

As the names flow on, I think about the nature of these ceremonies, concluding that they are somewhat like the player of the week in sports. Every team puts forward one nominee, who gains recognition. It doesn't matter if that individual did not perform up to the level of five players on another team. Every team is limited to one candidate and one only. After this mental dust settles, I feel better about representing my team, although I'm relieved that this process does not extend to a volunteer-of-the-year runoff. I'd finish dead last.

The city official concludes the roll call and introduces the mayor, who breezes in and quick-steps onto the stage. He is a survivor of the local political wars, a candidate I voted for. In mercifully brief remarks, he echoes his aide's words and moves along to the dog-and-pony phase. We are called one by one to walk across the stage to receive a pin and framed proclamation. After alighting from the stage, I see that the wording on my glass-covered citation imitates old English lettering and is overlaid on imitation parchment paper, a classy touch in my estimation. Also, some words are written in Spanish, referring to the mayor's office as "Oficina del Alcalde" and naming me a "Duque de Albuquerque." How about that? I'm an Albuquerque duke. At the bottom rests a fancy wax seal under the Spanish, "Haciendo Historia." Is haciendo the Spanish for seal? Hacienda is an estate. I make a mental note to look "haciendo" up. In the meantime these doings have cemented my newfound upward assessment of awards and citations and their attendant ceremonies.

I timed the event out at twenty-five minutes, evidence that not all bureaucracies are ponderous. One obligation remains, however. Each honoree must pose for a post-ceremony handshake picture with the mayor. This last exercise does not inconvenience me as I stare out at the photographer while my right hand engulfs the mayor's. But I sense that he is slightly ill at ease, and I think I understand why. The mayor is rather short and I am rather tall.

Interesting, is it not, that we employ the word "rather" as a euphemism? Someone is rather short. Someone is rather tall. Someone is rather needy. Someone is rather awkward. Someone is rather a jerk. The mayor, being a politician with the concomitant ego, may feel uncomfortable standing next to some cluck who is rather tall and who at this moment is overlooking the top of his rather low head.

Jennifer and Dennis collect me after my session with the alcalde, and we stop by the refreshment table before leaving. They express enthusiasm for my pin and certificate, and I acknowledge my debt to them and to the whole staff for their vote. And despite all the blather, I consider it an honor. Truly.

***

Weeks have gone by and Orlando is back. That's what Jennifer tells me, although I can't connect a face with the name.

"You must remember him, Fred."

"Sorry, no sale."

"I bet you'll recognize him when you see him. Anyhow, he needs a ride from University Hospital. He called and is waiting outside over there."

I roll into the hospital's pick-up zone where a grinning man, waving his arms, approaches the Ghost. Now it's all coming back. The face and name match. I welcome this recognition, confirming that I still retain faces in my brain's personnel file, if not names. Orlando sports a few days' growth of whiskers that dip toward a pointed chin, and he wears a cap with a Harley-Davidson emblem. The cap features a triangular peak at the front so that Orlando resembles an over-the-hill elf.

He opens the passenger door and bounces in with a, "Hey, how you doing, man? I remember you."

It's mutual and I say as much. "So what brings you back to the good old AOC, Orlando?"

"Oh, I had a stroke and some stuff happened and my legs are tightening up. They gave me some prescription pills. And I got to go to Social Security this afternoon at one."

That's what I call a pithy update. "You trying to get disability?"

"Oh, yes. I get six hundred a month now and that doesn't go very far. The rents around here are expensive."

Orlando speaks his second language in a way that carries a familiar ring to ears in this region. A lilting quality attaches to some spoken words as they are drawn out in mid-syllable. In this case "expensive" turns into "ex-PENNN-sive." I find this intonation melodic.

Orlando asks to go to Lomas and Broadway to pick up his "stuff."

The site lies a few blocks away from the direct route back to the center, and we make our way with ease toward the near-downtown. To our left at the designated corner stands an abandoned filling station-convenience store. Orlando points toward one side of the smeared-windowed building as we wait at a stoplight to make our turn. "There it is. It's over there," he tells me.

I glimpse a brown heap before turning and halting the Ghost at the debris-strewn far corner of the cement-block structure. To my surprise, I see a sleeping bag and backpack resting under a splintered plywood board half-covered with leaves. Orlando digs out his possessions, and I open the Ghost's sliding back door to welcome what I imagine to be his worldly belongings.

"How long were your things there, Orlando?"

"About five days."

I whistle. "Are you kidding? Why weren't they stolen?"

"Oh, I had my name on them. People on the street know me. They wouldn't take them."

"Really?" I have been taught a lesson about an honor code among the homeless. Reviewing the dispositions displayed by some of my past clientele, however, I have doubts about the code's universal application.

Orlando acknowledges taking precautions. "Well, I had a piece of cardboard under that lumber on top of them, too, but it blew away."

Orlando asks to make a run for something to eat. Also, he complains about being tired, jumping from that comment to the thought of canceling his Social Security appointment. Earlier, however, he seemed upbeat about it. All of this back-and-forth reminds me that in his previous incarnation with us Orlando had a habit of becoming disoriented, or manifesting that mental state in his comments.

After a fast-food stop, I leave Orlando at the respite door. I park the Ghost out front and climb the stairs to inform Jennifer about my conversation with Orlando and the contradiction in his wanting a Social Security appointment and now losing interest in it.

"I'll talk with him," she says.

Hearing this, I realize that I rarely witness business-like conversations between Jennifer and the respite men. Whatever she says, playing the part of a Dutch aunt, must be working because business tends to stay on track after her sessions with them.

***

Since yesterday Orlando has been joined on the ride list by Justin, a burly fellow with cropped blond hair topping a ruddy face. We are on the path to drop-off sites, riding along in silence until Justin mentions turning twenty-one last week.

That sets Orlando off. "I was in 'Nam' at age seventeen."

"I thought you had to be eighteen to get into the military." Justin says this but I thought so, too.

"No, my dad signed for me and I volunteered. He was career Air Force and thought that would be a good route for me." He displays a rueful half-smile. "I flew in a helicopter, but I had a choice. They wanted me to be a tunnel rat or a door gunner on a helicopter."

This is no time to give pride a free ride, and I ask for a "tunnel rat" rundown.

"Oh, those were guys who went into caves and underground places to root out the enemy. Because I'm small, they wanted me real bad to be a rat. But I wasn't about to go into those holes, so I got on a helicopter as a gunner."

"I guess you were stationed at the open door with a major-league weapon." Mental images of movie and documentary scenes from Vietnam help me out here.

"Right, an M60."

I ask for a translation in calibers.

"Seven-point-sixty-two millimeter."

"That ought to get the job done."

"Oh, you better believe it, man. They would tear a guy up."

I regret prolonging this conversation, although in a super-graphic way it has broken the silence.

Orlando is scheduled to visit an office at Central and San Mateo, but as we draw near he asks to be dropped at a corner three blocks away. "I know this woman. She has some money for me. I'll catch a bus later so don't worry."

I can't feature what Orlando might be doing with a moneyed woman, but deliver him to the designated intersection. "Good luck," he says to me when he gets out. I wish him the same.

Justin picks up on luck. "There's a lot of bad luck out there. But you have to trust life. I mean, if you didn't trust anybody you wouldn't get up and go out on the streets in the morning."

I chip in with another setting that concerns me when driving. "Right. And you surely wouldn't drive a car because you couldn't trust other drivers to stay on their side of the road. Not that they do all the time." (Or, when they allow grills to fall off their pickups.)

Justin shows that he is up on current events. "Yeah, but even walking around can be dangerous. I saw the other day that another guy got hit by a car downtown. And he was in a crosswalk. But the real killer story was in this 'Ripley's Believe it or Not' I read in the paper. There was this one guy out somewhere in the Midwest who got hit by lightning three times. Now, that's bad luck."

"It is. Maybe we could cut that guy some slack if he didn't go out of the house on stormy days."

Random rides again. Having no more to say about that ruler of ungodly mishaps, we move on toward Justin's destination, an office on Louisiana facing the Fairgrounds race track. He has been called for a second interview with the outfit, and he expresses optimism. "It's general clerical work, filing and answering the phone, and some billing. I need it because I have a bad back and feet. Physical work is out for me."

Siren blaring, an emergency rescue truck overtakes us on Central Avenue, and Justin says that he would not fancy hands-on medical work, although he might like to drive an emergency vehicle. "That I could do. But the stuff you see wouldn't be good. Especially the kids, the abused kids. I'd have lots of problems with that part of it." His mother runs her own private ambulance service, he says, causing me to ask myself why he is not staying with her.

But mother does not seem to be a player in Justin's future. "I hope I can get a job here in town and hang in at AOC a little while longer."

After Justin leaves me and I ride alone in the Ghost, I turn on the country classics station and reflect on what he said. Justin comes off as an engaging and sincere young fellow, and that gives me a fresh outlook because younger men, those under thirty or thirty-five, are infrequent inhabitants in respite. I cannot remember more than one or two others. The brutal truth is that the older guys are wearing out after hard times on the streets—if they manage to survive at all. They need security in their dotage.

Back in the center office, I report to Jennifer about delivering Orlando and Justin. We agree that Orlando is prone to change his mind about appointments.

She recalls that yesterday afternoon she had to prod him to go to Social Security. Orlando told her that he receives $1,100 a month in aid. "He paid into it for twenty years, he said."

I seem to recollect that Orlando quoted six hundred a month to me, but maybe he was referring to average rent. I'm beginning to doubt my memory. Or, I should own up to the fact that I am continuing to doubt it.

"By the way, Jennifer, Justin seems like a good guy. I guess he has some physical injuries."

Jennifer clouds over. "Suicidal. He jumped off a bridge but didn't succeed, if that's the word for it. So, he's got these terrible leg, foot, and back problems."

That explanation is not exactly a day-maker for me, although it explains Justin's physical limitations. I ramp up positive thoughts about Justin's landing his job. Yet despite wanting to block the image, I project all too clearly what action he might attempt if he does not.

Chapter TWENTY

Ben epitomizes a well-documented segment of the homeless universe. He holds membership in that populous group who fall asleep—pass out, if you insist—under freezing-weather stars once too often. He was not the first to do so and will not be the last. But Ben poses an extreme case. His feet were frostbitten to the degree that he has only half of his left foot and a stub of his right. After a protracted stay in the VA hospital, he awaits the arrival of special support shoes, or boots. In the meantime, he teeters around with a walker or, less frequently, in a wheelchair and questions whether he ever will walk on his own, special shoes or not. For now, he is shod in loose-fitting, cushioned slippers, blue-topped and open where his toes should be. White padding defines the outer edges.

Although I have encountered other toe-and-foot amputees, Ben ranks as the most enduring and endearing, besides being the worst off. He is self-effacing and well mannered to the point of being painfully polite, never more evident than when requesting a ride for supplies at Walmart or a checkup at the VA. "I can wait," is his mantra when I offer rides. "Take the other guys first. I don't want to cause anybody any trouble."

We are scheduled to visit the VA on this mid-fall day, accompanied by a high-backed wheelchair, complete with swiveling leg extensions. Because the old-fashioned chair supplied by the government can't be squeezed into the Ghost, I fall back on the disability-equipped white whale today.

Our journey falters right out of the gate. After helping Ben out of his wheelchair and guiding him into the passenger side seat, I attempt to load the empty wheelchair into the van. I open the Moby's side door and power the metal-mesh platform to ground level. I walk the wheelchair onto the platform, and then press the "Up" button only to have the lift stall in mid-air. I jerk the chair sideways and try again. No luck. I suspect that a sensor was offended by some protruding wheelchair part or other, such as the swinging leg extensions. Next, I seek to lower the lift—that's an odd expression—to start anew, but nothing budges. A deathly whirr rewards my effort. Not for the first time when dueling with "things," I engage in what the movie advisories describe as "coarse language." By this time, Al has been attracted to the spectacle.

Thanks to my long legs, I manage to leap onto the suspended lift platform. I would have entered the spacious rear compartment by slithering between the front seats, but Ben's presence on one side and the steering wheel on the other nullified that option. Holding onto the wheelchair, I bounce up and down on the platform while pushing the "Down" button—with predictable results. And for once Al cannot bail me out try as he might, a revolting development I greet with more coarse language. Al seems amused.

I seek out Jennifer, finding her upstairs in her office.

"We're going to have to call the tech about the wheelchair van. I can't get the blasted lift unstuck." I announce this in my most authoritative, mega-forte voice.

"Let me take a look," is her pianissimo reply.

As Jennifer sets off for the van outside respite, I corral my SUV out front and pull it around behind the white van. I am convinced—cocksure, in fact—that I will be required to put my own vehicle into operation to transport Ben. I take comfort by knowing that at least my rear hatch swings open and shut with ease, and that this feature will compensate me for gas burned on the roundtrip.

As I open the hatch, what I see elicits more colorful language. I have forgotten about three boxes of discarded books destined for Goodwill. Grunting, I unload the boxes, setting them next to the center's outside wall.

Looking across the driveway, I see Jennifer crouching in the van. I arrive on that scene at the moment she is pulling a foot-long metal rod from out of somewhere and inserting it into a slot out of nowhere that I had overlooked. Employing it like a lever, she pumps up and down a time or two, freeing the apparatus.

"There you go, Fred," is her lone comment as I attempt to be useful by pressing the "Down" button, redundantly warning her to keep her balance. Once lowered, she steps off the metal lift like the Queen of Sheba and disappears inside the respite area. I hope Al is taking mental notes to apply in the inevitable future crisis involving this "thing" and me.

Jennifer has saved the homelessness project a pile of money but not me from slight embarrassment. I say "slight" because during my lifetime, I have become more and more desensitized to humiliation when others—male or female, it makes no difference—master mechanical tasks that mystify me. Thus, without further comment, I position the wheelchair square on the lift deck, push the magic "Up" button, and hold my breath.

After the lift reaches its apex, I press the "Fold" button. The platform and chair slide into their proper locations inside the van. Why now? Perhaps this achievement was due to removing the wheelchair leg extensions and belatedly tossing them into the van.

What is that Biblical verse about wailing and the gnashing of teeth? To my credit, I have avoided the wailing part. So after I mutter a few more epithets under my breath, I gather myself and start the van.

Ben, of all people, apologizes. "Sorry. I know I'm a pain in the ass for you." He explains about needing the wheelchair. "The last time I showed up at the VA with the walker I thought they were going to have a cow. They don't want me putting a lot of pressure on what's left of my feet. So the walker is off limits, at least out there. Sorry about that."

"That's all right, man." I have recovered enough to feel ashamed of my outbursts, never mind my ineptness in dealing with the demon-possessed lift. I should be the one apologizing.

As we pull away and I become oriented to operating the whale van, I reflect about the circumstances leading to Ben's amputations, hoping to tease that story out of him. "So, I guess it was super cold around here last winter." I sense the obtuseness of my words.

Ben nods and runs a hand through sparse hairs combed straight back from his widow's peak. As I wrack my internal dialogue machine to crank out something more on point, he spares me.

"It sure was cold the night I got evicted at that place over in Tijeras." Ben recounts that he landed on the wrong side of the door after he and another fellow quarreled inside a mountain cabin. "I went outside and wasn't dressed for the cold. Yeah, I'd been drinking. It was my own damn fault. I've got no one to blame but myself."

I can't help but compare Ben's straight-from-the-shoulder analysis of his plight with Luther's cantankerous version of his. Remembering Luther, I talk about shoes. "You know, I drove this one guy around who had diabetes and he got special shoes that helped him a lot. They cost $2,000."

Ben gives out with a low whistle. "I think they said mine would be $500. It could have been more."

Conversation never drags with Ben. Like the Energizer bunny, Ben bounces from one topic to the next without running down. "I really want to get out of here and get a job. Maybe a waiter, if my feet could stand it. My advisors don't think I could do it. But I tried to get a job before all this happened. I went to every restaurant on Central. But they just want to hire kids, you know, young types. But at least I had a resume all printed up. So when they asked for one, I was ready. I think I fooled them."

Abruptly, he turns to his quest for Social Security disability. "I' going to meet with my social worker so I can get some help with the application. Then I'll make an appointment. Supposedly, the paper work takes 90 to 120 days. Supposedly. At least that's not as bad as the appeals backlog, from what I hear."

I add that from what I read, Social Security disability appeals take almost a year on average.

"Yeah, it's unbelievable. And they get you going and coming, anyway. Did you know that for a family of four to get food stamps they have to make less than $26,000 a year?"

No, I did not know that. In keeping with my vow to adopt a simplified lifestyle in retirement, I try to ignore the red tape complexities tied to public assistance programs. Such language makes my head hurt. And aren't I lucky to be in a position to ignore them?

Ben continues. "I was talking with this guy the other day and he can't get any more benefits, even though he's disabled. They say he earns too much. I mean, God forbid someone should be comfortable in this life. No, no, we can't have that."

I am at a loss for any comeback to Ben's unexpected prickliness. Not to worry. Ben still is wound up.

"I guess that's why they killed Kennedy. He was for the people. He wanted to help people so they killed him."

Ben is revealing a darker side today. I am not only at a loss for words but also for thoughts, although I suppose Ben's take on the Kennedy assassination, featuring the ever-popular "they," is not any nuttier than any other crackpot conspiracy theory clogging up public discourse. I venture to ask if any subsequent president has championed the downtrodden.

"Not that I can see. Since then, eight or nine presidents or whatever, all of the money we need here at home is going overseas. Don't get me wrong. We ought to help those people when we can, but we have too many problems here in the good, old U.S. of A. right now."

Before I can summon a diplomatic response, Ben leaps another wide chasm, subjectwise. "Hey, I don't want to cause you any trouble. I know you're a volunteer and all. I really appreciate what you do."

I trot out my pat reply. "Don't mention it. This is what I do to steer clear of boredom in retirement. My wife likes to see me out of the house some, and this place sort of grows on you. Besides, I'm only here two mornings a week. It's not a burden. Really it's not." And that is a fact, despite my earlier whining episode.

The VA complex sprawls before us like a college campus, although like my visits with Norman and others I circumvent the warren of outbuildings and stop at the main hospital entrance. The entry is unusually crowded today with veterans coming and going, many with halting gaits and accompanied by companions who I figure to be either spouses or sons or daughters. Like me, some might be volunteers.

I guide Ben down from his perch and he steadies himself on the open passenger door while I negotiate the intricacies of lowering the wheelchair. All goes well at first as the chair reaches ground level, and I help Ben into the seat before retrieving the leg extensions. One snaps in easily, but the other won't cooperate. I try positioning it with great care, but it falls to the concrete walkway with a clank. Some hospital visitors sitting on outside benches appear unduly interested in my labors. I snort outwardly and swear inwardly. I'm sweating. I resort to putting on my reading glasses, a move that advances the task, leading to a welcome click as the leg extension fits into its slot. I smile at Ben.

He smiles back. "Sorry about causing so much trouble. The next time we go out, except here, I'll use the walker."

For the second time this morning I am humbled. Good lord, Fred, the man has no feet and here you are having reached the Biblical three score and ten, walking around without even a limp and enough retirement income to allow you to gallivant all over God's creation.

I try to salvage a shred of dignity. "Ben, forget it. I get a kick out of doing this, and you're a good guy. My problem is that I tend to get mad at things, but I try not to get mad at people, and for sure I'm not mad at you. I'll see you later."

He nods and wheels away after assuring me that he will find his way back to the center.

When I pull away I imagine Ben inside the hospital's vast waiting area. Although I do not visit the innards of the hospital often, I've been in there three or four times to pick up respite men. It's not an uplifting sight. Veterans young and old sit around biding their time. During a holiday-time visit I witnessed their being serenaded by a mariachi band that to my ears succeeded mainly in adding melancholy to the scene. Some vets seemed alert enough, but others sat trance-like. A good number were in wheel chairs. I recall one fellow with a missing leg. Those using walkers did so with varying degrees of mobility. Many were shuffling along.

Reviewing this scene, I conclude as I have before that those Washington types who send young men and women into combat should be required—by law, no less—to visit a veterans' hospital preceding their collective decision to formalize a war, or a "police action," or "preemptive strike" or whatever term constitutes the flavor of the day. Does the official terminology make any difference to those who get killed, or who survive with debilitating physical and mental problems? And my proposal goes double for "wars of choice," masked in the vernacular as "preemptive military actions." Now that I think about it, why not mandate that all war supporters serve four hours a week, a mere half day, in a veterans' hospital for the conflict's duration. Thoughts such as these make me long for elevation to king for a day. Stand back, America, for a flood of controversial decrees from the royal palace.

I recollect a report I did in eighth grade on *All Quiet on the Western Front*. When my teacher, Mr. Meyers, debriefed me, he asked what solution the author, Erich Remarque, suggested through one of his characters to relieve the masses from fighting wars. I came up with the answer. One German soldier proposed that in place of conscripting other people to fight, the leaders of feuding nations should be equipped with clubs and gathered into a big ring where they would fight to the finish. The country represented by the surviving statesman would be declared the war's winner. I would like to have proposed my own ideas on the subject to the late Mr. Remarque, and flatter myself that he would have approved.

Arriving at home base and without riders, I swoop into the front parking lot. Inside, I meet up with Dennis heading upstairs. I see him infrequently, although his office is situated next to Jennifer's. He keeps busy at his desk or attends what appear to be an endless series of outside meetings. I hope Dennis will follow my lead and write off meetings in retirement.

"I've got something for you, Fred," Dennis says, motioning me into his office.

Although he is a generation and a half younger, Dennis and I share a geographical bond. We have discovered that we grew up in towns about fifteen miles apart in eastern Indiana. My small hometown is Winchester and his Selma. Like me, Dennis got out and about in his youth, roaming the country. Somewhere he made an acquaintance who wanted to keep in touch but had forgotten Dennis's name. Then one day, a letter arrived at the home of Dennis's parents addressed to "World Traveler, Selma, Indiana." Good luck with that delivery in a big city.

Dennis is fresh from another trip to Indiana where he visited relatives. He talks about his visit, and with a broad grin presents a charcoal-gray baseball cap.

I burst out laughing. Across the crown of the cap are the words, "Nothing Tips Like a Cow—Indiana." The profile of a supine cow is stitched on one side.

Discussing cow-tipping, Dennis and I deny that we ever engaged in that shady activity, although we had heard whispers about it. Maybe it's a myth, like snipe hunting. Who knows? But the thought does stimulate the imagination. Goats would seem to be easier prey, I think, although unlike cows they might be able to right themselves.

After thanking Dennis for my new cap and negotiating the stairs on my way out, I think about Ben and compare his predicament with that of my old bantering mate, Joseph, "Little Joe." This thought paints a third layer of shame on me today. Joseph has a "bag" that no one wants. Ben lacks two feet, which everyone wants. And here I am with no bag, two big feet, and a minimum number of potholes encountered on life's highway.

Outside in the front parking lot, I become panic-stricken. Where is my car, my very own gray ghost? It's nowhere in sight. Well, why not? Having it boosted would put the cherry on the whipped cream of this day. Then from a recess in my cranium a faint beep emerges. In a huff, I had pulled my car around to the space outside the respite door, where it was not needed after all, thanks to Jennifer's fixing the wheelchair van lift.

There it is, although I discover that the good fairy has neglected to put the three book boxes back. I lug them into the car's rear compartment, resisting the temptation to engage in more colorful commentary. I congratulate myself on my forbearance, but admit that the temptation had penetrated to the conscious level. Well, take your little victories where you can. A minor improvement in one's conduct is better than no improvement at all, so I'm told.

Chapter TWENTY ONE

Ben needs, or wants, a lift to Walmart. He gives me a crooked smile as he approaches on his walker. "How's it going, Mike?" This misidentification stuns me. Maybe he never tried to call me by name before. I forget. I correct him and he smiles sheepishly. "Sorry, Fred."

"That's all right. But I thought you were supposed to be in a wheelchair."

"Naw, that was just for the VA. I decided after all the hassle last week with the big van and all that, from now on I'll use the walker, even at the VA. I mean, what are they going to do to me, amputate my feet?" He laughs at his gallows humor. I don't.

Far be it from me to enforce VA guidelines, and the bald fact is that Ben's using his walker allows me to pilot the Ghost and not the Moby wheelchair van.

Joining us on our venture will be "Mr. Holbrooke." To my knowledge, Mr. Holbrooke is the first respite resident to be known to the staff—and by extension to me—as "Mister." His appearance contributes to this bow to formality. Pale blue eyes punctuate his tanned weathered face that is noticeably unlined. His hair hangs long and straight and snowy-white, balanced by a spade-shaped flowing beard that swipes the top of his chest. He also carries a plastic bag hooked up to a catheter. Except for that appendage, he reminds me of the character Ben Gunn portrayed in the Wallace Beery version of *Treasure Island*.

Mr. Holbrooke has a bank appointment today, self-scheduled, because he is hell-bent on having a banker straighten out his account, although I suspect it is Mr. Holbrooke who needs straightening out. Jennifer reports that he suffered a disastrous trial run yesterday. "It didn't go well."

Stoop-shouldered, Mr. Holbrooke moves at a snail's pace with his walker as he joins Ben and me outside the respite door. Mr. Holbrooke wears a loose-fitting windbreaker to help conceal the bag that at the moment registers all but empty to my prying eyes. He insists that I drop him at the bank's main office before I take Ben shopping. Mr. Holbrooke is a man I cannot deny.

Meanwhile, I have taken an order for Camel cigarettes from Tim, a former furniture mover nursing a bad back. Tim smokes unfiltered Camels. "My mother told me not to smoke, but if I was determined to do it, smoke unfiltereds. She was right. All that silicone and junk in filters will kill you." Now there's a relative argument. Tim gives me eight dollars in ones for a pack. I also take an order for hydrogen peroxide from a new resident whose name I don't catch, although he catches on that I am headed to Walmart. "Get a little bottle. I use the stuff to soak my feet." He points to his mottled feet resting atop flip-flops and then hands over two ones.

With my two riders and two take-out orders, which I commit to paper rather than to memory, I drive toward downtown. A parking space opens up near the entrance to Bank of the Southwest. That's lucky. And I mental note myself for the umpteenth time to lobby for a handicapped placard for the Ghost, although helping Mr. Holbrooke to step down from the van goes well. He is careful to grasp the plastic bag as he settles onto the pavement where he pauses to stash it more deeply within his floppy coat. I hold the bank door for him, assuring that I will be back in due time. I assume Mr. Holbrooke is a known quantity at Bank of the Southwest.

Ben and I travel to Walmart to the accompaniment of Ben's monologue, punctuated by my responses in clipped sentences. I ask about his shopping list. He recites items that include coffee, creamer, soft drinks, and TV dinners. I remind him that the AOC supplies coffee and powdered cream.

"I know, but I want to help carry my weight, make a contribution. I've got the money."

At the store, Ben commandeers a self-propelled cart, setting his walker in the prow of the basket like a spinnaker sail. He executes a nifty 180-turn as he heads off, saying, "Wow, this thing turns on a dime."

I seek out a certain clerk at a middle register. She is a jolly sort and has humored me and the men before. She is a great one for repartee, so I announce that I'm buying the cigarettes for somebody else. She places a forefinger perpendicular to her lips. "I'll pretend I didn't hear you," she says, lowering her finger. She chides me, explaining that the law forbids third-party purchases to prevent cigarettes from falling into the wrong hands, such as minors. "One of the clerks got suspended for three months for doing that." She gestures toward a supervisor patrolling the aisles.

Uncharacteristically quick on the uptake, I size up the situation and proclaim in a hearty voice. "Yes indeed, I've smoked straight Camels all my life. I love these babies. Those filters are for the birds. Lots of junk in them, you know, but these fags are made by tobacco men, not medicine men. They're killer smokes, so to speak, packed with the finest burleigh. Yes indeed, I'd walk a mile for a Camel." I wink at the clerk who registers appreciation even though I grossly have overplayed my hand. Her shoulders heave and she winks back as we complete the transaction. Whether she remembered the ancient Camel slogan about walking a mile, I'll never know.

In the pharmacy area, I spot a small bottle of hydrogen peroxide on sale for a dollar. Taking into account my earlier luck with the bank parking space and this deal on peroxide, I consider playing Powerball. This is shaping up as a lucky day. Clutching the peroxide and the cigarettes, I walk to the building's opposite end where Ben sits second in line to check out with his treasures. No trip to Walmart ever passed so smoothly—almost.

A snag develops with Ben's debit card. He was confident that his balance totaled twelve-hundred dollars, but the checkout clerk gives a negative shake of her head when she looks at her screen.

This sequence takes me back to another clerk who shook her head at a screen. It happened a generation ago in Amarillo at a Texaco station where my wife and I stopped for gas, and where true to my nature I sportingly decided to forgive the great Texas oil giant.

In my mind, Texaco needed forgiveness because its credit card operatives tried to stiff me. Specifically, those pirates tried to charge me interest on an offer that I declined. It involved a typical come-on deal from yesteryear, in my case a thirty-dollar annual introductory offer for a car club membership. So I fell for it, taking comfort in the fact that I could cancel without penalty within thirty days. I did so. But the next thing I knew, an item on my credit card bill showed a seven-cent interest charge based on the thirty dollars that I canceled.

Naturally, I returned my payment minus seven cents, with a most cogent and diplomatic note pointing out the company's error. No reply was forthcoming. Memory fails, but as I recall this song-and-dance went on for a few months with the interest ballooning to eight cents before I gave up on the card. Take that, Texaco.

So some months later in Amarillo I was low on gas when what should appear but a sky-high Texaco sign by the Interstate. Well, why not? Let bygones be bygones, I thought. I'll be bigger than a bloated oil giant and deign to throw my business their way again. Thus I landed in front of a clerk and proffered my long-idle Texaco credit card from a neglected corner of my wallet. That led to the remembered head-shake after she swiped my card for a second time.

"I can't understand what's going on, sir," she said. "This card hasn't expired, but the machine won't take it. I can't explain it."

"Oh, I think I can," I said without missing a beat. "Here, let me pay you in cash."

To this day, I remain of two minds whether the mega corporation or I prevailed in our titanic struggle. But guess where I do not buy gas anymore?

Back in the present, I fear that Ben's card has expired because he mentioned not using it for two months. But the problem is that Ben has two hundred less to spend than he figured. He shrugs philosophically. "Guess I forgot something I bought. Who knows? Who cares?"

After loading the Ghost and pulling away from the store's loading zone, I pry into Ben's finances.

"Yeah, I got regular Social Security coming in, but like I said before I still need to go for an appointment for the SSI." He sighs. "At least I got Food Stamps.

They have the Food Stamps set up better now—a card. And the form to fill out is down to about seven pages." He says this without a trace of irony. "And that E-Z tax form, it's only one page. So, you don't have complications. Anybody can do that."

Ben, however, has not had a wrinkle-free history with the E-Z form. "But one year, I had money coming back and they took it for some hospital bills I had. There went that dough."

I would appreciate finding out how a hospital or similar business can garnishee a federal tax refund, but decide to leave that canine snoozing, although Ben's delivery makes his anecdote compelling. I inquire about his feet. "Are you any better balanced now after our trip to the VA.?"

"Not really. I need my shoes for that, the ones with braces. They're still talking about four to six weeks, but you can bet that will turn out to be four to six months."

To facilitate matters, I drop Ben back at respite and help unload his goods before collecting Mr. Holbrooke. Ben asks if I will be around tomorrow.

"Yep. I'm in here Wednesdays and Thursdays. I'll see you then."

"I hope so. I just remembered I forgot some stuff at Walmart that I'll need to get through the weekend."

Questioning—but not asking—what more Ben could need, or want, I deliver the Camels to Tim, who nods in appreciation when I give him the odd change from his eight dollars. He heads outdoors immediately, tearing the cellophane off the cigarette pack as he goes.

The man with flip-flops livens up when I hand the peroxide to him, plus a dollar. He is impressed by the low cost. He inquires about the sales tax, and I tell him to keep the dollar. It's easier for me that way, but I appreciate his asking.

I wave an all-encompassing goodbye, thinking that I should have asked flip-flops his name. Maybe I have been engaged with too many men and names in the last few years, leading my inner computer to run a procedure that cleans my hard-drive files in some fashion. I suspect that my analogy would give a computer geek a hearty laugh.

Pulling into Bank of the Southwest lot, I spot Mr. Holbrooke waiting outside the entrance. I approach him and notice that a yellowish liquid is swirling toward the top of his bag. I fear that he has been inconvenienced by a long wait, but he chooses to complain instead about not achieving any satisfaction from his visit. I volunteer to bring him back tomorrow and accompany him inside.

"That's good of you," Mr. Holbrooke responds. He does convey a dignified manner somehow, befitting his formal title.

***

Some days bring unexpected assignments. Some do not. Today there is no surprise when Jennifer reminds me to take Mr. Holbrooke to the bank. "You know that things didn't go right again yesterday with him. I think he needs a statement or record of some kind. He can't understand where his money goes."

Ben has canceled his trip to Walmart with a cavalier swipe of his hand, so I have to take up the conversational slack by promoting a conversation with Mr. Holbrooke as we drive along. He responds to my question about his predicament, although I avoid mentioning the bag with its yellow liquid.

"Protective custody." If it's possible to spit words, Mr. Holbrooke is accomplishing that. "Yeah, the cops took me in and then I ended up with that crazy, frickin' doctor."

"Where was that, university hospital?"

"No, no, no." I have exasperated Mr. Holbrooke, who corrects me in an upper-register voice. "Over at Health Care for the Homeless. That fool doctor just looked at me and told me I had health problems—didn't run a physical on me or nothing."

I would like to hear the doc's side of that get-to-gether. My contacts with Health Care for the Homeless and the personnel there have been uniformly positive.

Inside the bank, I match Mr. Holbrooke's walker pace as he inches along. We are intercepted by a gatekeeper who recognizes Mr. Holbrooke. "I saw you here yesterday," she says. "Wait here and I'll get someone for you."

A smiling man, short and compact and dressed in a crisp business suit, strides toward us, and I take the initiative, explaining that I am with Mr. Holbrooke who is having trouble with his bank balance.

We are motioned into a glassed-in office where I slip into a chair next to an inner wall, leaving the outside chair for Mr. Holbrooke and his baggage. We must present an odd couple to the man I assume to be "Mr. Chavez," given the name on the desk plate. On second thought, I am casual enough myself, sporting leftovers from yesterday's shave. Perhaps I ought to spruce up more when I deal with bank types.

The banker introduces himself as Mr. Chavez. From the start he seems to be a good-humored sort. Perhaps he specializes in hard cases. "What can I do for you, gentlemen?" I refer him to the bank statement held by Mr. Holbrooke, adding that Mr. Holbrooke has trouble understanding why his balance was fifty-four cents yesterday. Mr. Chavez takes the document and types on his keyboard while alternately staring at his computer monitor. He explains that he has pulled a statement from the past month, and with that done and explained, all becomes clear. That is, all becomes clear to me and Mr. Chavez but not to Mr. Holbrooke.

The gist is that $457 in Social Security benefits are deposited into Mr. Holbrooke's checking account on the second Wednesday of each month. Mr. Chavez notes, and turns his computer monitor around to display the numbers, that Mr. Holbrooke uses a debit card to withdraw the full amount, typically on the same day. Also, owing to some past time lag between deposit and withdrawal, an odd fifty-four cents was available yesterday, although that was cashed out. I suspect that a frustrated teller tired of explaining Mr. Holbrooke's account status to him and forked over the change, leaving a zero balance. The next Social Security deposit will take place in a week, Mr. Chavez informs us.

The bank officer is accommodating beyond call. He mentions that he sees Mr. Holbrooke in the bank regularly. I ask about the last withdrawal because Mr. Holbrooke keeps repeating that he can't understand who is taking his money. After a few minutes Mr. Chavez returns with a hard copy of the transaction showing that Mr. Holbrooke indeed withdrew $457 the same day that his last Social Security deposit was posted. I look at the document, asking Mr. Holbrooke whether that is his signature on the withdrawal slip. He nods. And I wink at the helpful bank officer. Why am I winking? Does that represent some feeble attempt to distinguish myself from the man I am accompanying? Am I saying, however unconsciously, that I'm not one of "them?" I hope not, although I would not be the first to think or say that. Every now and again one of the men, in a most confidential tone, informs me, "You know, Fred, I'm not like the other guys in here."

I thank the bank man and arise, clueing Mr. Holbrooke to do the same. After a pause he stands as I notice that his bag is well concealed beneath his jacket.

Outside, I attempt to reassure Mr. Holbrooke that all has been explained, that he is taking out money as soon as it comes in and thus has no balance until the next Social Security money arrives. He is not buying it. I say that I will tell Jennifer about our encounter with Mr. Chavez and that perhaps she will want a copy of the statement and withdrawal slip. Mr. Holbrooke responds that he still wants his money. Now, I'm the frustrated one, but I try to hide that.

Mr. Holbrooke's coat front has parted, and before I return him to the center I notice that the liquid in his bag is approaching the upper half. Back in respite, he makes his way to his bed and plops down on the mattress edge, instructing me to instruct Jennifer to see him "ASAP." Why does she have to be bothered, now that I have taken care of this matter? I settled this issue most efficiently, didn't I? Yes, that's my ego squawking.

I inform Jennifer about our bank visit and Mr. Holbrooke's continuing confusion over his account. "He needs to see you right away," I say in a mock commanding voice.

She grins. She knows I'm bluffing. "Oh, yes, Mr. Incharge. I'll get on that right away."

The thing is that she will do it, reminding me

that she and others at the center go about their business for forty hours a week, often more. In contrast, I'm on call four or five hours a week. And I understand, as I have many a time, that I should undertake the proverbial attitude adjustment to better imitate the center staff's even-tempered nature.

Chapter TWENTY TWO

Ben's approach to conducting business at the Social Security office differs from most people's, mine for sure. He is determined to drop by there today. This shaves two days off the date set for his disability appointment, meaning that it's take-a-number-and-wait time. Besides bypassing self-pity, Ben impresses me with his self-reliant streak. "I don't have much use for appointments. I figure if I go there in person I can move things along better."

Perhaps. Because Ben already has prepared a sheaf of forms, he may beat the system. On the other hand, forms seem to present extraordinary hurdles to Ben, one in particular. "They want a certified copy of my birth certificate from California." That document is essential in securing Social Security disability, that grail quest among my men—and why shouldn't they apply? By any fair-minded definition, almost all qualify as disabled.

I inject some politics into the birth certificate issue. "Sort of like Obama."

"Yeah, Obama." He opts to bypass commenting about the president's difficulties with "birthers," instead complaining about bureaucratic barriers. "I knew it would be complicated, but I didn't know how complicated."

We are riding with Ray, a self-styled wizened veteran from the streets and, to hear him tell it, of multiple bureaucratic campaigns himself. Ray's swarthy appearance is accentuated by a coal-black Fu Manchu moustache, and he talks in the manner of a smug old hand adept at surviving life on the margins. He will be let off at the New Mexico Human Services office to request state General Assistance. He asks Ben for a form they discussed before we set out.

Ben rifles through his papers, muttering. He and Ray are displaying elevated signs of impatience. "No matter," Ray says. "I can get one some place else. I just thought you had one."

This challenge spurs Ben to greater machinations of paper shuffling, and soon he emerges triumphantly, holding a single sheet above his head. "Here it is. I knew I had it." I'm pleased to see Ben put the ball into the end zone at least once this day.

After saying goodbye to Ray, we snake our way across the parking lot sandwiched between the state and federal offices.

Ben anticipates a future battleground. "Yeah, General Assistance, that's what I was trying to think of a few days ago, General Assistance. I need to get started on that, too, I guess. I'll look into it."

Why does not qualifying for Social Security disability automatically suffice for state assistance? Also, the term Social Security seems inapt. It provides welcome income for us retirees. But despite its title, Social Security often fails to provide full security. As for social, my experience is that many beneficiaries are not at all social. Before I drink too deeply at the bitter terminology well, I call a halt to thinking about this potential blood-pressure buster, recalling my vow to finesse details about these subjects. After all, I promised to keep my life simple and carefree in retirement.

Outside the Social Security entrance, Ben worries about a return ride. He speaks about taking a bus if

I don't show, although we both know that is unrealistic given this side-street location off the bus route and his relying on a walker rather than a wheelchair. I doubt that he is serious, a doubt confirmed when he asks, "Will you be around until eleven-thirty, Mike?"

I correct him again about the mistaken name identification, and he apologizes all over himself. But why should I be surprised or offended? The respite men are exposed to shifting scenes populated by a duke's mixture of staff and volunteers. I suspect that I would confuse names and faces in their position. As for a return ride, I suggest that he call Jennifer if I'm gone.

"No, that doesn't work. Jennifer doesn't answer her phone."

"Can't you leave a message?"

"I can, but that doesn't work either."

We settle on my guaranteeing to return about eleven, after my scheduled run to aluminum recycling. Back at the center, I mention Ben's fears to Jennifer.

"He doesn't trust voice mail, so he won't leave a message. He just won't. So, I can't work with him on that."

Sigh.

Nervous about keeping my pledge to Ben and Ray, I rush through the visit to aluminum recycling and with relief note the time, ten fifty-five, when I pull into the Social Security lot. Inside, I tell a security officer that I am looking to pick up a "friend." The word slipped out naturally, and upon reflection "friend" reflects an honest way to describe my relationship with Ben, despite his name confusion.

"What does he look like?"

"He's easy to spot. He has half of each foot amputated and wears blue-colored slippers. But he's using a walker, not a wheelchair."

The guard smiles. "Oh, yeah, he's been around here all morning." He motions toward the assembled throng where I see Ben positioned in an aisle chair about half way up the waiting room. He is reading a book.

"Oh, there you are," he greets me. "Hey, everything went smooth today. I got my papers in."

"Did they check them over?"

"Only a quick look . The guy said everything was okay and that after the birth certificate comes in, all I need to do is wait four or five months. That's what they told me, but you never know about that."

"Well, Ben, all things come to those who wait." Ben responds with a grimace.

We ride across to the state office where Ray is outside smoking, a bent leg propped against the tan, textured wall. He plunks down into the rear seat without comment.

"How'd it go?" I ask this sensing that there was no go.

He pushes air between pursed lips. "Oh, they need some more forms. It took me an hour to find that out. I think I need a lawyer."

I must be some relation to Pavlov's dog as this stimulus triggers remembrances of Curtis and Norman and others who enlisted lawyers to lobby for public benefits. I relay this information to Ray.

He seems interested. "Do you know what they charge?"

"I don't know exactly. I do know that these lawyers specialize in Social Security cases, but you would think that they could branch out and do something about state General Assistance. Seems logical to me."

That information seems to give Ray hope. Placated, he asks Ben about his morning, and Ben takes that ball and runs with it, all the way back to home base.

As I am signing out at the front desk, I hear the swish of a broom, and then see the broom, and then Al. I ask how he is faring these days, as in, "What's up, Al?"

"Oh, good, Fred. I got a new place. It's down on Broadway, way better than my old one."

I would imagine so. The entry into Al's old apartment—a word that employs the term loosely—looked like a vintage college dormitory with narrow, dark, hallways. I never saw his room or rooms and didn't care to. The exterior was enough. "What's it like."

"Oh, it's a brown stucco building that sits by itself at the back of this guy's house. I moved my stuff in there already, but I don't have a bed."

Passing up a query about what contrivance he was sleeping on in his old apartment, I ask, "How do you sleep now?"

"On the floor, in a sleeping bag."

Once in a blue moon the stars align, coinciding with a burst of light illuminating my brain. In this instance, I remember that my wife and I are scheduled to bring new beds back from my mother's place, freeing up two frames and mattresses now occupying space in our guest room for, well, Al for one.

"You know, Al, we've got a couple of surplus beds over at our house. One's yours if you want it."

"For real?"

"Sure, we can pick it up tomorrow when I come in, or after I take any of the respite guys."

"Fred, you're all right."

"Hey, Al, I'm the man."

This elicits Al's routine infectious laugh. Al and I have our lines down pat. Perhaps we should consider expanding our repertoire to pursue a stage career—strictly county fair level, I must admit. At least we would laugh at our own jokes, and everybody else be damned.

***

On the way to pick up Al this morning, I think about his existence. Here he is the custodian for a men's shelter where day after day he sweeps and cleans the dormitory, presiding over dozens of beds—seventy-one plus six, by exact count. Yet he does not have a bed to call his own. How can anyone reconcile that?

No respite riders were scheduled, so Al and I are making for my house to load up a bed frame, mattress, and box spring. He gained permission to commandeer a couch from the center, a couch well beyond its "best-if-used-by" date, which we stuffed into the wheelchair Moby after pulling out the lone bench seat.

My wife and I have positioned the bedding and frame inside the garage's automatic door, so I back the van into the concrete driveway for easier loading. Hopping out, Al surveys our front yard, graced by pine trees, uniform-and-edged grass, and rose bushes.

"You got a nice home here, Fred."

The word home is not lost on me. "We do. I know I'm lucky to have it."

I punch the buttons on the key pad and the garage door wobbles upward to reveal Al's prize. "Wow, this is a nice one here," Al says, stroking the quilted mattress.

Al seems fascinated with our manicured subdivision, which a postal carrier dubbed "Pleasantville." It could appear that way, although I believe we have our allotment of unpleasantness, given occasional break-ins, barking dogs, and bothersome cats running wild.

Al responds in detail when I ask how he's commuting to work from his new location. "Oh, I take a bus and then catch the van that drops the men downtown in the morning. But not today. I slept in today." He reports this with a subtle grin.

Al is wearing a ski cap in place of his trademark baseball cap. The cap and his features echo those of the Inca descendants I observed decades ago in the Peruvian mountains. Perhaps a racial connection exists in the mists of time. Back to real time, I ask my usual question about how his quest for a new ID is progressing.

"I still haven't gotten that. I might get a driver's license, but I'd probably go out and get a DUI."

I ignore the negativism. "Did you ever have a driver's license?"

"Oh, yeah, I had one in 2000. That's when I got out of my marriage. I don't see her anymore. It's best that way. She went to Salt Lake City."

Al believes that divorcees are better off cutting the ties that once bound. "No, you need to get away. You hear about too many guys who still see their wives after the divorce and they assault them and all that."

He has a point. "Do you have a child?"

"One." Al is turning taciturn.

"Boy or girl?"

"Boy. He lives with his mother."

"Do you have any contact with him?"

"Just by telephone. I need to get in touch with him soon."

"Is he in school?"

"He's 29. He's what you call self-employed."

No percentage in pursuing this topic. Anyway, Al is giving me directions about making a right turn and then a left to reach his new residence. Unlike the apartment farther up the street, this location in the city's South Valley presents a more residential setting. But unlike my subdivision, no shade trees grace the sun-baked brown stucco facing the street or the one in back where Al indicates to pull in. We do so in a cloud of dust.

We reverse the loading processes for the bed and couch. The angle through a narrow outside door proves daunting in negotiating the couch, but we manage it. Lurching through the doorway, I am greeted by a landscape strewn with odd-shaped boxes and clothes and sundry possessions. The room is square with an open door to the kitchen and beside it another opening to a bedroom where a sleeping bag lies across the floor. We clear a space for the couch.

Next comes the box spring. "Go ahead and lean this up against the wall, Fred, I'll set the bed up later." Al has fashioned a cramped clearing for the bed. We repeat our movements, leaning the mattress against the spring and the metal bed frame horizontally to brace the pair. Despite a calendar day in November, we are enjoying balmy weather and my shirt has become sweat-stained.

"Looks like you have the makings of a good living area, Al." I did not mean to make that sound like mockery and hope Al did not take it that way, considering the obvious upgrade.

"Yeah, it's quite an improvement on that other place."

We close up the wheelchair Moby and with a bounce pull onto the street, leaving behind the dirt driveway that is indistinguishable from the front yard. Al looks over at me and offers his thanks, followed by his mantra. "Fred, you're all right."

"Hey, Al, I'm the man." County fairs, here we come.

Chapter TWENTY THREE

My fellow volunteer Kay—she of the bedbug battles—intercepts me in the parking lot when I arrive at the center. I haven't seen her in months, and I ask whether she was subjected to the VA security check. Obviously, I have a fixation on that nightmare.

She rolls her eyes. "The stuff at the VA itself—even finger-printing—wasn't too bad, but that online form was a bear. I hate those dumb things, but thank God for Brian. He got me through it."

Misery loves company. Indulging in brazen self-pity, I relate my adventure.

Kay reacts to my tale with a rueful smile. "Keep your chins up, Fred."

I check in and pick up one ride request, from a new resident, Sean. Before I get the lowdown on Sean, I inquire about Ben. He tops my current list of people to fuss about.

Jennifer frowns. "He's gone."

"Oh, no. He wasn't ready." I had grounds for fussing about him, it appears, although last week he impressed me as operating on an even keel, even talking about the pending arrival of his shoes.

"One of the social workers saw him at the Smith's at Tramway and Central, old 66, and he was rolling out in his wheelchair with a case of beer in his lap. I tried to get word to him that he could come back, but he hasn't shown up."

"Did he get his new shoes?"

"Evidently not. Maybe he has them but likes to use the wheelchair to haul beer around."

Although I don't kid myself that I'm in the soul-saving business—assigning that undertaking to those harvesting in another vineyard—I do aspire to promoting the men's physical lot. And Ben's lot could have been improved if he had persevered long enough to be fitted with support shoes. I would like to track him down, but I can't stake out Smith's hour on end on the off-chance of meeting him. That's what I tell myself.

Because they rode together, I link another resident to Ben. "What about Mr. Holbrooke?"

"He left for Colorado. We haven't heard from him."

The center residents' turnover continues to wear on me, more so than ever with Ben's departure. Names and faces blur, signaling that I might become less human by distancing myself from emotional ties to them. In short, I fret about becoming callous to the men's fate and, by extension, to others' fate. As a potential counterweight to that, the new man, Sean, awaits me.

Jennifer recites the *Reader's Digest* version on Sean. "Sean's an interesting guy. He played football for the Raiders. That's what he said."

If I can't get energized by interacting with a former professional football player, I ought to take a sabbatical to recharge corroded batteries.

Sean is easily identified in the respite unit. He is brawny and from the waist up built like bricks piled on top of one another in ever widening rows. I beat him by about two inches on height, but otherwise flunk out in the physical presence department. His hair is jet black and he sports a pencil-thin moustache. He appears to be

pushing middle age. I introduce myself and we go outside to board the Ghost for university hospital.

"Jennifer tells me you played pro football."

"Yeah, a little."

"Where?"

"Oakland."

"Before that?"

"I went to a small school, Illinois Wesleyan."

"I heard of it. I'm from Indiana." That doesn't
draw a response, nor should it. "What position?"

"Defensive back." This information confirms my
mental image of NFL players' enormous size because
Sean's build resembles that of high school and college
linemen in my day. Now they're defensive backs—and
speedier.

Silence rides along, and I can't devise any way
to overcome that. Sean comes off as polite but scarcely
gregarious, even a bit aloof. Despite my intentions, however, I can't resist another question. "So, how long did
you play?"

"Long enough to ruin my knees but not long
enough to make it for a pension."

I frown. Sean's predicament underscores a long-
held impression. "I read something about that. Anybody
working on a deal to let ex-players like you qualify? I
know that the baseball pension clock starts running
within a couple of months after a player makes the bigs."

Sean shrugs. No doubt I have blundered into
mine-field terrain. Returning to Plan A, I drop him at
the hospital without further prying. "If you get out by
eleven, give a call."

"I'll be out all day after I get through here.
Thanks, anyway." Limping, he makes his way toward
the double door.

Driving back to the center, I imagine Sean meeting Al Davis, the prickly Raiders' owner, and would love to be treated to anecdotes about that. But the way our relationship is not progressing, I doubt that Sean and I will exchange many confidences.

I make a detour to buy disposable razor blades at Walmart. Jennifer mentioned that the supply has run out. I pay $2.60 for a packet, which I chalk up to a donation. Even shaving seems to have an angle with the men. I am told that when intake staff members hand out soap, shampoo, disposable razors, and shaving cream, they squirt a dollop of the shaving cream into a paper cup, rather than surrendering whole aerosol cans. "They just disappear," Jennifer says. Anyhow, I have accomplished my extra-good deed for the day, in case anybody up there or in any direction is bothering to tally. It's not as though I'm bucking for volunteer of the year.

Back indoors, I turn the razors over to Jennifer. She responds with appreciation and asks whether I have time to help out in back. Sure.

She leads me to the storage room where clothes lie in disarray around the sorting and laundry-basket area. I thought I had seen the worst back here, but it appears that either someone turned up mad or drunk, or both, and started flinging objects about mindlessly. A half-full coffee cup rests next to a wrinkled washcloth. Blankets are strewn over a stack of shirts awaiting hanging. Pillow cases cover the sorting table. Blankets and sheets intertwine in the sorting cart.

"Yikes, so what tornado ripped through Albuquerque last night? I must have slept through it."

That draws a Jennifer smile. "Well, we can't say. It was some of the men looking for clothes probably.

Who knows?"

She departs for her office and I survey the mess in greater detail. Then I mount my ever-faithful high horse, granting that this outrage-burner ignition is turning into a tiresome habit. But why should the royal "we" tolerate this sorry behavior when "we" have other tasks on tap? A basic tenet of the center holds that the men be treated with respect. And we do, staff and volunteers alike. I've been around long enough to vouch for that. Yet does not respect run both ways? A two-way street? Where's the respect for us and our time?

Tethering my steed, I get down to work, starting with long-sleeved shirts, befitting seasonal cold weather. More than a dozen shirts lie about, and after working them into hangers I reach over my head to plunk them onto a metal pipe running above the one reserved for slacks. My height proves an advantage. Then, pants are sorted, and underwear and socks stuffed into their proper homes, metal pigeonholes, but not before I uncover a black flashlight. It's a substantial one, heavy, with a barrel long enough to contain what I guess to be four fat batteries. That discovery throws me. Who left that lying around?

Al walks by and we commiserate. "I don't know, Fred. What are these guys thinking of? Howard had everything sorted out in perfect order."

At least my fellow volunteer has been spared this chaotic scene. I ask Al if his space was violated. "Anything of yours messed up?"

"Oh, yeah. I found my dust pan over by the sheet shelving. Somebody went over the top, I guess." Al expresses this with a shrug.

When in doubt, consult Jennifer. I find her up-

stairs and report that the once-strewn space has been re-
stored to a state approaching normal. I repeat Al's comments and put in a plug for him. "Al doesn't need that."

"No, he doesn't. I'll look into it."

I notice that she has been eyeing the flashlight in
my left hand. "Jennifer, what do you make of this thing?"

"Well, Fred, it's a flashlight." A puckish smile
accompanies this long-overdue putdown. "Seriously, it's
like the ones the night security guys use. I guess one of
them forgot it. Maybe he went back there with one of
the men to get clothes and got called away."

Bottling up my impulse to call for a congressio-
nal investigation to complement Jennifer's local inquiry,
I set the flashlight on her desk and check out.

***

Wednesday morning kicks off a new volunteer
week with less than a promising prospect. Sean needs a
ride to Walgreen's to fill a prescription. Our time together should not be saddled with incessant talk. But when
Sean swings into the Ghost's passenger seat, he catches
me off guard by initiating the conversation. "They told
me you're a volunteer."

"That's right. I've been doing this ever since I retired. It keeps me out of trouble." I ought to come up
with a new line for that response, but it suffices, excus-
ing me from deeper thoughts about why I and others
volunteer. I'll work that out some day when Dr. Freud
comes to town.

Although I'm watching the road, I sense an attitude adjustment upward in Sean. I suspect my status
as a volunteer was responsible. I test that by poking into
details about his disability.

Sean does a quick take on his downfall. "I got a knee blown out and never could get back up to speed. Then the other one started giving me trouble, so I had to give it up. And then some bad stuff happened and here I am."

I don't turn onto the avenue leading to "bad stuff" but start talking about Raider teams and Al Davis. That kindles a string of stories from a talkative Sean. My curiosity has been satisfied.

At Walgreen's, Sean is in and out in minutes, but when I back away I come within an eyelash width of plowing into a parked car out of my rear-view mirror's range. I slam on the brakes with a curse. A man on the sidewalk stares at us and I stare back. Sean and I burst out laughing. The man still is staring. Sean and I may not be brothers in the bond yet, but we're gravitating into the same orbit.

He asks to visit Goodwill to try on clothes. For a moment this request raises the possible conclusion that he was the offender in the back room last night. But Sean's reference to Goodwill concerns me more. A visit there would not be my choice, owing to a previous episode.

Dropping off spare clothing at Goodwill one day, I spotted men, women, and children clustered around a side entrance. With no immediate assignments, I walked over and was informed that I had arrived at "Clearance Corner" and that a "call" was coming up at ten. You take a number, and when it's called you are permitted to jostle your way inside and load up whatever you can carry, paying by the pound. Why not join the crowd?

I secured a number, somewhere in the sixties as I remember. Then the cattle call began, with a harried worker hollering out numbers. I slipped through impatient people blocking my way when my number came up and stepped inside. Bedlam.

People were rushing about pell-mell, snatching items from yawning gray plastic bins and stuffing their treasures into bulging sacks. I figured a good number of such items would be peddled for resale around town. Fearing that I might be trampled, I found refuge away from the storm, stopping at a safe distance to survey all manner of worn household utensils, grubby appliances, and tattered books, among the hodge-podge meriting the label "junk." No one seemed attracted to the bookshelves where I lingered less than a minute before failing to find my own treasure and fleeing. Outdoors, I was relieved to inhale fresh air. Again, I was reminded that the sensitive, the vulnerable, and the faint-hearted are not cut out for life on the streets or at their curbside margins. Nevertheless, many have no choice.

I relate this past episode to Sean who agrees with my suspicions about the "junk" and its destination. "Oh, yeah, I saw that mob once. What gets taken out of there turns up in a lot of garage sales around town. Sort of like recycling."

I suggest an alternative site to Goodwill. "You ever been to Thrift Town? It's got better goods as a rule than Goodwill." This is not a fabrication, although Thrift Town represents a more convenient destination for me. In fact, I have shopped the place many a time, accumulating such goodies as smart-aleck T-shirts—one proclaiming across its front "Titanic Crew"—two belts, and three wine glasses.

Sean is amenable. "No, but let's go check it out. I'm getting an upgrade on my wardrobe. I may be settling down here. You know, I used to get all my shit on a single clothesline strung up across a room. All I had to do was roll my clothes up, put them in a bag, and off I'd go."

That low-maintenance life strikes a romantic chord with me. I'm verging on vicariously envying such a happy-go-lucky existence on the road when I snap back into reality and picture the dreary street life accompanying that existence. No, in my final-glide stage I'll take my overstocked bedroom closet and the lifestyle represented.

At Thrift Town, Sean shops for trousers, pulling three pairs off a rack before carrying them into a plywood fitting room. I wander around cadging for bargains and seize upon a beer stein for a dollar.

Walking to the cash register, I witness the door to Sean's fitting room swing open for some odd reason, revealing him in his boxer shorts. I glance at his knees with the X-pattern scars from surgery. The door is closed and soon Sean emerges. "These will do, I guess," he says, cradling two pairs of trousers. "This place is a little on the high end, though."

Again, relativity hogs the limelight. To me, the prices here cluster at the low end.

Walking to the van, Sean asks to move on to Goodwill. Why not? Like a take-charge guy, he directs me street by street to the outlet on San Mateo where he alights. Heading back to the center, I picture Sean during his pro football career, shouting instructions to his cohorts in the Raiders' defensive backfield. I would like to have been a fan in the stands to see that.

***

At home and curious, I go online to check Raider rosters from seasons that ought to include Sean's playing days. I checked with Jennifer for his last name, a name that is missing from any roster. Whether this omission can be chalked up to Internet unreliability, to incomplete information from the Oakland football franchise, or to Sean's imagination, I am and will remain an agnostic. Maybe he was on a taxi squad or similar back-up group. Maybe he played parts of several seasons. Maybe, maybe, maybe. But after all is said and done, does it matter? Should it make any difference to me, making a cameo appearance in Sean's life? He looks the part, acts the part, and knows his lines. If he has a need to exaggerate whatever role he played in football, that's his business, not mine. He has the right to narrate his life story. I don't.

***

Sean is raring to go this morning. He hails me in the parking lot for his last ride. His backpack and duffel bag are chock full, and we fling them into the Ghost's rear seat.

"Home, James." Sean laughs at his command as I fire up the van.

"You're in a good mood. Guess you've got a right, what with checking out of the AOC and coming up with a home away from here."

"Oh, yeah. I've got a setup going for me down on Zuni." He looks my way and winks, leaving me to conjecture about the Section 8 housing awaiting him.

Sean navigates our journey, directing me over streets I think I know by heart. But I figure that performing this function empowers him, and I will not deny that to him or any man in his position, any more than I will question Sean's professional football credentials. He and others like him are powerless enough already.

"Go on down to Gibson," he tells me.

If we are destined for Zuni, this amounts to heading south to go north. But I check myself, and proceed as directed, keeping my vow to avoid control issues. I try to pry information from Sean about his new berth, but he turns tight-lipped. "Oh, you'll see," is his response as we turn onto Zuni. "It's just past the next light. It's the place that was a gas station."

I identify it, a filling station converted into a storefront church. "City Heights Mission" reads a hand-lettered, white-on-black sign.

No sooner have I coasted onto the cement apron separating the mission from the street than a woman bolts from the door. She wears ruby-red lipstick and a body-hugging white sweater. Her coal-black hair matches Sean's in color but not in length. Her hair hangs below her shoulders. She flashes a mouthful of gleaming-white teeth.

Sean bails out of the Ghost while we're still rolling. He and the one-woman greeting committee collide in executing an embrace. I worry that the woman might be Sean's last tackle. They kiss longer than your standard cousins and waltz away, arms intertwined around waists. Sean does not look back.

I go around to the van's side door and unload his belongings and call to him. He turns to offer a slow, arcing wave. So long, my friend. I do hope that you are "set up" for a long spell because you are fulfilling our agency's independent-living goal, albeit not in the conventional way envisaged by our exit planner.

Chapter TWENTY FOUR

Ben died.

Weeks ago when the news got around that Ben was back on the streets, I muttered under my breath, "Dammit." Now I amplify on that to Jennifer, who has delivered the bad news, "Damn it to hell." She says Ben was picked up unconscious on the streets and taken to the VA hospital where he didn't survive. For all practical purposes, he died on the streets despite his hospitalization.

So it has come to pass that meek-and-mild Ben, who dreamed an impossible dream of becoming a waiter, and who never wanted "to cause anybody any trouble," caused terminal trouble for himself. Although I don't suppose that Ben had the wherewithal to consider the fallout from his death, he also has troubled me. I suppose his passing provides one way, the hardest way, to confirm that my dedication to the Albuquerque Opportunity Center and its inhabitants is alive. I wish Ben were.

Conceding that "deserve" is a highly-charged word when linked to human activity, I contend that Ben deserved a better fate, or at least a better end. Yes, yes, he fired off a gilt-edged invitation to Mr. Trouble to drop by sometime, and Mr. Trouble will always and everywhere RSVP in the affirmative. Yet, I can't shake the thought of Ben's dying alone, except for uniform-clad strangers hovering over him in an institutional bed. Or, could he sense their presence?

I ask for details.

"We don't know much," Jennifer says. "Veterans Affairs called about it. Ben was found unconscious somewhere out on East Central. He lasted no more than a couple of days at the VA hospital."

"What did he die of?"

"They won't say. Probably something related to exposure. He had to be in pretty bad shape."

I fear that he was, and block the temptation to dwell on Ben's condition when he was picked up. And why couldn't he have left us in warmer weather. Again, I'm playing "I wish." I prefer to remember a smiling and spruced-up Ben, and at intervals even a Ben contemplating his future.

Life and rides lie ahead. We must roll on. Daniel and Randy have requested rides. They are new to me, and I ask Jennifer for thumbnail sketches.

"Daniel is a talkative guy. He's a Native American, or at least enough so that he goes to the First Nations health center. I think he's a Northwest or Alaskan Indian. Randy is an Anglo guy with a big bandage on his left hand. He's trying to get Social Security disability. He's going to see a lawyer who specializes in that."

This detail recalls anew chain-smoking, oxygen-sucking Curtis, who sought legal help to qualify for Social Security disability. I figure that Curtis's image is burned into my memory.

Downstairs I look for a Native American. I can't detect such an individual among four men breakfasting around a ping-pong-sized table, so I stick my head outside. Nobody in sight. Back inside, I call toward the breakfast club for Daniel. A heavy-set, pink-cheeked fellow nods and allows that he is Daniel. Ah, another stereotype demolished. But honest-to-Pete, he looks more like an Irishman than my standardized mental picture of a Native American. He is full-bearded, no less. Maybe before I depart the planet I'll get it through my noggin that culture trumps race.

Randy raises his concealed bandaged hand to complete roll call. His ringleted brown hair protrudes from under a ski cap. I introduce myself by first name and tell both men to finish up at their leisure while I bring the Ghost around to the respite door.

Later, once under way, I appreciate the full meaning of Jennifer's adjective "talkative." In a voice associated with alcohol and tobacco invasions of the vocal chords, Daniel sustains a monologue to rival a cable-TV evangelist. He occupies the back seat during his lecture. "Somebody said you were a teacher at the University of New Mexico, Fred."

"That's right."

"I know about UNM. I was going for my architecture degree there, just to formalize what I'd been doing all along. But then the requirements changed and I was looking at eight years instead of two. Of course, the idiots wouldn't grandfather me in, so I quit. Then my girlfriend got pregnant and that was the end of my academic ambitions."

Although memory falters on specifics, I know that somewhere along the line I have been treated to variations on this theme.

"I still kept working at designing buildings, though. I designed an office building where Broadway crosses I-25. You've probably seen it. It has board-and-batten construction with vertical four-by-tens. It was a little restaurant with office space upstairs, and the property owner liked the effect so much he built up the whole property that way."

I am about to ask for a mini-seminar on board-and-batten when I become distracted, unable to find the lawyer's precise location on Lead near Yale. If you ever have to rely on a driver to deposit you within shouting distance of a given location, I'm your man. But if you need to be delivered to a specific doorstep without incident, I'm not your man. In this case the problem arose when Lead was converted into a one-way. A section where it curves forms the equivalent of an oxbow lake, a short dead-end cut off during the changeover. Daniel spies an opening that we just sailed past. After squaring the block to reach the office, we squeeze into a space that once defined the front yard of an adobe-style house. Randy makes for the office-house.

Daniel and I settle in to wait. I ask Daniel about his medical issues.

"Oh, I got throat and mouth cancer."

I rue the crack about his vocal chords. "What kind of treatment?"

"Both chemo and radiation. Actually, they had to stop radiation around my mouth because my skin was falling off. I felt sorry for myself until the doc reminded me that the same thing happens to guys with prostate cancer."

Getting the picture all too graphically, I shift topics. "Got any children?"

"Two, but they don't live here. I'm not in touch too much. No, my wife and I divorced, and I found out that the one who has the money gets the justice. She had an inheritance, but she got most of everything anyway. Of course, it didn't help that I didn't show up for the hearing."

No doubt. "So what did you do after that?"

"I ended up working construction on a ranch, three-hundred a month plus room and board. And then I got the Big C. No health insurance, of course."

After twenty minutes, Randy returns, reporting that he will come back once the lawyer finishes paperwork. Now, he needs to visit University Hospital for a checkup.

Daniel hits the resume button. "I was telling Fred here about my cancer, but I didn't mention that my chemo is called recombinant mouse DNA."

"Mouse?" I ask. "That's a new one on me."

"That's what they called it. I always wondered what effect that might have on my system long term."

Randy has an answer. "I don't know. Maybe your nose would start twitching."

"Good one, Randy. As a matter of fact, it's starting to tingle right now."

Maybe these two should cast their lot with Al and me on our county fair circuit. Swallowing that thought, I refer to the bandage imitating a pinkish mitten on Randy's left hand.

He describes a ball of fire that overwhelmed him when a gas stove exploded inside his Arizona trailer home. "I'd been living over there in a fifth-wheel for a long time. It was a good place. I put a pizza in the oven and popped outside to get some fresh air. When I came back and opened the oven door, the fireball came. I heard this noise and saw these walls of flame coming toward me. Blew out the sides of the trailer and roof. That's all I can remember."

Could a negligence or product liability suit be relevant here? Maybe Randy's seeing the wrong lawyer, but I honor my pledge to avoid practicing law without a license. "You must have had lots of other burns."

"All kinds. Multiple skin grafts and all that. It's a good thing I'm not black."

I jerk my head in his direction.

"Don't get me wrong. What I mean is that if I was black, my face would be pink-and-white-streaked from the burns and grafts. I know. I saw some of those guys. As is, I'm lucky to have my nose, but my ears sure are thinner."

Daniel cues another anecdote. "Tell him about what happened to you over in Arizona."

"All right. Well, there was these hippies coming across my yard. They were high on something and decided to go shopping at 2 a.m. and cross my yard to do it. I scared them plenty. And, you know, those bastards went to the law on me, every single one of them. And so next thing I knew I was down at the cop shop facing all these charges. Then the DA's office offered a plea deal. There was a lot of pressure to take it. They said that if I'd plead to one, they'd drop the rest and put me on probation. Otherwise, they'd bring me up on all the charges in court and I might go to prison. So, I took the deal."

"That seems like the logical move under the circumstances." I realize that my words are failing to provide any solace.

"I guess. But the police came and took all my guns except for one, the cheap one. They took a couple of them that was worth $2,000 each. I'd been collecting guns ever since I was eight years old."

I'm struggling to process Randy's saga. From reading between the oral lines, I presume that Randy waved one of those $2,000 guns at the "hippies," although that detail—and God knows what else—was absent from his narrative. What about the gun that was left to him? Did it melt in the fire? Is the fire the reason for his being on the streets? I'll check into that and other particulars another time, maybe. At the moment, I'm suffering from autobiographical overload.

All the while, Daniel has been directing me around the University of New Mexico campus as we wend our way to the hospital on the far side. He dishes up a Cook's tour, although I taught at the place for eighteen years. I remember Sean's back-seat-driver directions, from the front seat, and employ my same rationale to Daniel's instructions. Losing one human GPS but gaining another suits me. Pride aside, I need the help—sometimes.

Because no parking spots are open when I pull in at the hospital's front entrance, I block cars along the curb where a driver instantly becomes anxious to get under full steam. He lays on his horn while Randy departs.

Daniel joins Randy as the honks continue. "I'll sit around here a while and catch the shuttle on the way back. Thanks for the ride." After Daniel shuts the rear sliding door, I move forward in the driveway at a record-setting snail's pace. Mr. Honker tailgates me—much to my enjoyment.

Doing my paper work back in the center's parking lot, I turn over more than two pages in the Ghost's log book. As a rule, a page and a half are completed, maximum, before the gas tank needs refilling and the sheets carried inside for record-keeping. The gas gauge registers more than half full, indicating that someone forgot to remove the log sheets after filling up, or someone donated a tank or partial tank. With gas prices flirting with four dollars a gallon, I discount the latter.

Of more personal and immediate concern, however, is that some nincompoop has run off with the Ghost's ballpoint pen, forcing me to get out, walk across the parking lot, unlock the center's front door, go inside, liberate a pen from the front desk, go back to the Ghost, and enter the mileage, date and places visited, along with my initials, then retreating to let myself inside the center again. If the extra bother seems like small potatoes, unbecoming a so-called adult, try it for about the fourth time. I resist, heroically, the urge to take the pen back inside with me. No guarantees, though, about my conduct following the next earth-shaking, filched-pen caper.

A new chore awaits. Jennifer informs me that to relieve overcrowding in the downstairs' file cabinets, inactive resident records dating back more than three years will be pulled and boxed up for the archives. She unlocks a four-drawer cabinet—one in a line of six—and points to a yellow tag marking where a previous sorter left off, close to half way through the "Fs." This shapes up as a tedious task, prompting me to attempt weaseling out by playing the privacy card. "Are you sure a volunteer is supposed to have access to these?"

"No problem. There might be with the current residents, but not the past ones."

Culling the folders presents no challenge, merely opening them to locate the intake sheet date. Minor complexities arise when a man has returned for a second or third visit, but the work becomes routine. I am about to wrap up my morning when I pull a folder holding a picture photocopied from a newspaper. The moment-in-time attracts my attention. The photo shows a spic-and-span young man, suit and tie and slicked-down hair, shaking hands with an older man who looks important. The cutline informs that the young fellow is being congratulated by a U.S. congressman for being appointed to the U.S. Military Academy at West Point.

Precipitous falls from promising futures happen all the time, I know, but I can't help but speculate that the life story that unfolded between the picture's publication and the not-so-young man's street life in recent years would yield an absorbing memoir.

***

I'm back in harness after a two-week vacation in Hawaii, feeling almost guilty about the double life I lead. Chuck, a new resident, has scheduled a ride, but when I seek him downstairs he is AWOL. My Irishman Native American, Daniel, is still with us, resting on his bunk and I ask him about Chuck.

"I'm worried about him," Daniel says. "We were taken to First Nations last evening and Chuck never came back. There are a bunch of guys over there who like to carouse."

Left to my own devices, I wander out into the main dormitory where a blast of hot air washes over me. I greet Al, performing his sweeping and mopping chores. Al acknowledges me with his standard greeting. "Fred, you're all right," followed by my standard reply, "You're the man, Al." Mutual laughs bring down the curtain on our patter.

Al preempts my observation about the temperature. "How do you like the heat in here, Fred? That's because they fixed the dampers. I got the thermostat turned down, but it's going to take a while for things to get adjusted right."

Where is Goldilocks when we need her? I heard last winter that the dorm tended to be too cold, now it's too hot. Considering the money spent on the heating-and-cooling system, that climate control breakdown seems implausible. But Al launches into an explanation about metal bars positioned the wrong way inside the ducts, preventing the dampers from opening fully. He adds that a crew from the installer came around to fix the screw-up and didn't charge. "It was their fault. So we shouldn't pay."

I should say not. Saints preserve us, operational dampers would seem to be an essential part of installing heating ducts. Exercised, I mention this later to Brian, who was unaware of this most recent foul-up. He sloughs it off. "We've had lots of problems with those guys."

This is turning into a running joke. I gear up into high dudgeon about some vexation or other while the staff accommodates to an imperfect world and moves on. In these matters but not all matters, I should move on as well.

After reporting Chuck's absence to Jennifer, I take the Ghost for an overdue visit to the Octopus car wash. Last week the local paper reported that a woman worker was killed at this site when a vehicle driven out of the wash spun out of control. She was among those assigned to towel off clean cars, but as the victim of some impossible-but-true sequence was pinned against a cement block wall. The story lacked details.

In the Octopus waiting area I spot a snapshot showing a smiling woman wearing a quilted jacket and jeans. Apparently taken at the site, the colored photo has been affixed to a window looking out onto the workers' area. Under the picture on the eight-by-ten sheet are the words "In Memoriam" accompanied by the victim's name and lifespan dates. I calculate an age of 24.

Forgive me for using that word, deserve, again, the judgmental one overworked when summing up random acts, both good fortune and bad. But I'll trot it out now because the deaths of the young woman and Ben tilt toward opposite poles defining the deserve continuum. Depending upon one's worldview, Ben shouldered either the entire burden or the greater share of it for his demise. He had choices. But the minimum-wage woman wiping down cars in the open air in blazing heat or stinging cold, was not responsible to any appreciable degree for her death. She did not send out gilt-edged invitations to Mr. Trouble. She did not have a choice. She deserved a better fate.

Chapter TWENTY FIVE

Albuquerque's First United Methodist Church is gussied up for the Christmas season, garlands gracing the nave near the altar and poinsettias abundant. Joy to the world. But joy is not the mood that has prompted me and others to gather downtown today. We have come to remember the homeless who died on Albuquerque's streets this year. We mourn them.

I sit alone in an uncushioned wooden pew and open my program to the alphabetical listing of the dead. Toward the bottom I locate the name I knew would be there: "Ben Stang." Ben has been gone for many weeks, but this black-letter confirmation aggravates an old wound. I wish I could have found Ben after he left the center. I wish I had made an effort. I wish a lot of things.

Having sat through two previous memorial services, I know the drill. First, we will hear from the Rev. Trey Hammond, a Presbyterian minister and an Albuquerque Opportunity Center founder. He will recite bleak facts about homelessness and conclude with a call to action. Then the homeless will testify. This open-microphone portion will kill up to three-quarters of an hour, but is time well spent. Then overhead lights will be dimmed and candles lit before the names of the dead are read aloud by single individuals, as prearranged. Next, unlisted names will be called out from the shadows, bringing the final toll to about seventy. Lights will be turned up, a song will be sung, and we will file out. I will go quietly, bypassing the refreshment table. No socializing for me here.

The timing of the event is symbolic. The calendar date marks winter's official start, the day of longest darkness, a daunting condition on the streets.

As the Rev. Hammond stands, I size up the crowd. I sit three rows from the back and notice that Jennifer and Dennis are stationed about halfway between me and the platform. I count seventeen pews split by a center aisle, each pew seating up to eighteen bodies across. Although not packed, the sanctuary could be classified as full. I estimate close to two hundred souls on hand.

After a prayer, the Rev. Hammond opens the nondenominational service by noting that Albuquerque is among one hundred and twenty cities across the nation holding similar events under auspices of the National Coalition to End Homelessness. Then he launches into his message, which seems to have graduated from the no-holds-barred school of oratory.

"It is unacceptable that so many die on the streets in the most prosperous nation on earth; it is unacceptable that 200,000 of our veterans are homeless; it is unacceptable that another 200,000 children are homeless each day. These truths are an indictment of our society."

The facts pile up. Life expectancy for a homeless person is under 50, twenty years less than the average. The homeless are three times more likely to die from disease than the housed. About half the homeless live in family units. Almost forty percent of the homeless are afflicted with significant mental problems. In Albuquerque at least thirty-two-hundred women and children are without homes every night.

The minister's rundown makes an end run around unrelieved gloom, however. He praises the city's new initiative, "Albuquerque Heading Home," which identified 75 homeless men for paid-up public housing. Linked to a national program, "Heading Home" aims to address the core of the homeless issue, housing. That may belabor the self-evident, but housing first has not always been the strategy. "Heading Home stands the traditional approach on its head," the reverend says. "Before, you had to rehabilitate yourself and jump through hoops before you moved into a place. Now the emphasis puts housing first. You move in and then go through the support services."

This strategy appeals to me, and I regret not taking part in the hundreds of street interviews that identified those seventy-five most medically vulnerable homeless men. I excused myself on the grounds that the interviews took place in the wee hours. Yet the mayor himself—a new one, not the one who presented my award—pushed the effort and took to the streets to do his duty on an unseasonably cold night. My thoughts are interrupted by the obligatory ring of a cell phone echoing through the space.

A piano solo comes next on the agenda, followed by poetry readings. One poetic refrain in particular hits home. "You ask me why I'm homeless. I stubbed my toe, I stepped on a tack, I got caught in a net, and it was all downhill from there."

It's time for testimonials, and I count sixteen men and woman lined up to take the stage. They are reminded to limit their time to two minutes, a request that often has gone unobserved and mercifully unenforced in past services.

Some speakers focus on religion. One man reads Scriptures, crediting God for overcoming an alcohol addiction. Another recollects being saved by God and talking with Jesus.

One fellow relates a conversation with a local preacher. "I asked if he believed in God, and he said, yes. Well, I said, then you are homeless.

"I'm not homeless, the preacher said to me. I have a four bedroom house in the Northeast Heights.

"No, I said, if you believe in God, you're homeless, because you're not home until you get to heaven." After a smattering of laughter, the storyteller continues. "You know, that preacher asked me if he could use that one in his next sermon."

Applause breaks out after a woman reports being homeless for seven years and sober for fourteen. The kicker in her story is that she was sober before she was homeless. Applause also commends a statement by a man reporting thirty years of sobriety.

Others plead for the community to support the homeless, respecting them as individuals. The phrases are heartfelt. "We are seen as body parts on the street," says a middle-aged man. "Names not statistics" offers another. I could have contributed the Metropolitan Homelessness project's motto, "Criminalizing acts of survival is not a solution to homelessness."

Countering the religious testimonials, one fellow dares the exhortation, "No more spiritual masturbators," before pleading for more community involvement.

Some sing their thoughts, including a near-professional performance of "Amazing Grace." Alas, a flat-riddled rendition of John Lennon's "Imagine" falls a country mile short.

Some break down when remembering the death of a friend. One speaker provides a dose of whimsy. "Homeless people are some of the happiest people you'll ever meet." The speaker pauses. "But it may have taken them two or three years to get there." A live-wire participant wears a Santa Claus cap and looks the part in beard and girth. He rambles about his life and an old friend, but comes up with a pithy line about people with housing. He asks them to imagine arriving at their front doors, turning their keys in a lock, going in and looking around, and deciding whether "you need all that stuff." He adds, "You have a home. You are blessed by that alone."

A standout to my liking is a chap appearing to be in his twenties. He admits to a drug problem and speaks in slurring but highly-charged syllables about his existence. He recalls being told by a passerby to "get to work." The young man's reply: "Being homeless is work." The audience response to that zinger would max out an applause meter reading.

Lights are dimmed, candles lit, and names called. I count sixty-two in the program. A man three rows in front of me reads Ben's name. It's just as well that he was called upon to do that and not I. When the list is exhausted, the appeal goes out for additions, drawing seven more names. By my count, more than a half dozen of the dead are women. Precision is impossible because along with Sandra and Anna come such ambiguities as Kim and Lee.

After silence blankets the church, we close by singing "Sunshine on My Shoulders." The "Art Street All-Star Band," a homeless aggregation, accompanies. I leave without approaching Jennifer or Dennis.

Appropriate to the season, it's twilight and the winter wind slices through my unlined wool jacket.

Owing to the crowd, I have parked two blocks away from the church, and break out in shivers before I reach my gray SUV for the drive home. I am comforted physically and mentally by the passenger compartment cocoon, and rather than turn on the country classics station, I consider the homeless. I need silence for this. Tonight, of all nights, I wish them to be sheltered, and to see one more light of day come morning.

Streaming in my mind, I match names and faces of the homeless who have paraded through my life and then vanished: Curtis and Luther and Little Joe and Don and Orlando and Jim and Norman and Ben, along with others not as vividly remembered. Except for Ben, their stories are incomplete, as far as I know. I represent a fragment of their life span. Even their pasts are sketchy in most cases. For example, I never knew and will never know about the events that took 79-year-old Jim to the streets. He "got away" before I could hear his full story. Through Jennifer, I know that Norman is ensconced in the veterans' home in Truth or Consequences. But the meandering life paths pursued by the others will remain uncharted in my mental atlas. Are they all sheltered this night?

Shelter. Many who serve the homeless deem the word to be too limiting, too much treating the symptom and not the cause, too much the Band-Aid and not the comprehensive remedy. To a degree, I concur that shelter alone reflects an attitude and goal from former times. I make a positive association, however. If I were on the streets this night, shelter would be my primary concern.

After pulling away from the curb, I realize that one of my proudest self-images has been a deception, a mirage. I suppose that a stickler for unvarnished honesty would call it a lie. My choice, however, leans toward the

euphemistic. Until coming face to face with human beings lumped into the category "homeless," I would have
challenged anyone who said that I had enjoyed a sheltered life. Not I. In fact, I had prided myself on kicking
around the world in my youth, and later undertaking
major changes geographically and professionally. But
the reality is that I always and everywhere had someone—family and friends—to catch me if I fell, stubbed
my toe, stepped on a tack. Someone always was around
to secure my safety net. I never lived on the edge, let
alone in the abyss.

True, in college days I had washed dishes one
summer in the Rocky Mountains and waited tables
on the Virginia coast the year after. These adventures
occurred after the summer I dug ditches alongside
blue-collar "lifers" employed by my hometown natural
gas company. Toss in Peace Corps deeds in Chile and
six months' teaching in the Philippines where I was tick-
eted for an unwanted ringside seat to an attempted military coup, with side dishes involving general assignment
reporting at a metropolitan newspaper, a professorship
at a black university, volunteering at a food pantry, and
my adventures at the Albuquerque Opportunity Center,
and the old cross cultural resume reflects a citizen of the
world. Or so I thought. But when I ran into homelessness defining the lives of others, I realized that I never
had to worry about a roof over my head or the source of
my next meal—with meaningless exceptions. The bases
and basics were covered. Home was always a sure-fire,
taken-for-granted destination.

Home. The word pulls on our psyche like few
others. From "The Odyssey" to "Home Alone," from the
sublime to the ridiculous, the striving to return home or

to protect a home has supplied storytellers with wagon-loads of fodder through the years. Our literature and popular culture are replete with references to home, and even those who have endured life in a bad home seem to yearn for a good one. The word encompasses a felt need, a sentimental longing that cannot be quenched when you are away from it or, worse, when you have lost it. To butcher the mother tongue, when you are without a home you are "less a home," and thus to some people's thinking you are less of a person. Homelessness relegates you to living under the sun and stars or under bridges with the dangers attendant to that survivalist life. You are a portrait on the negative side of the home coin. And what if your old home place is inhabited by folks who don't care to take you back? Often for valid reasons, I admit.

Adages about home march into my consciousness. "There's no place like home." Or, the syntactically challenged, "Home is the place where if you go there, they have to take you in." (I assume that my old junior high English teacher, the sainted Miss Ford, would carp about Robert Frost's daring to end a sentence with a preposition.)

The associations continue their flow. "Home Sweet Home," "home run," "home plate", "Be it ever so humble there's no place like home." The refrain from George McGovern's 1972 Democratic National Convention speech: "Come Home America." "Make yourself at home," and the Spanish equivalent: "Mi casa es su casa." "The sailor home from the sea, the hunter home from the hill." Edgar A. Guest, the newspaper poet: "It takes a heap of livin' to make a house a home." Finally, a personal favorite, "Home is where you can scratch where it itches." I've gone too far.

On occasion I sing in the car, almost always when alone. And I never have subjected my respite men to this imposition. But thoughts about home invoke words from the old gospel hymn, a staple of altar calls, "Mercifully, Tenderly, Jesus Is Calling," and I feel compelled to belt out the refrain while at a stop light. "Come home, come home, ye who are weary come home." I'm rather impressed with my effort, until I realize that I am gesturing with one hand, like a choral director, as well as singing. I sheepishly glance to my right. The driver in the car alongside is a woman young enough to be one of my middle-aged daughters. Mercifully, she's staring straight ahead, but I appreciate the stoplight's changing to green anyway.

No one is immune from losing a home. I lost one this year. Not the Albuquerque one I live in, but the one I grew up in, my Indiana home. My mother died, and as the only child I acquiesced to selling the house that had been home to our family for four generations, a two-story frame structure built by my great-grandfather, a Civil War veteran. My father was born there and died there. At birth I was taken home there from the hospital. Nevertheless, all concerned agreed that it was "time" to sell, given my distance from the place. So my home has become a house to me. My only home, at last, is where my wife and I live. The lifelong, out-of-state competitor is somebody else's home, and that is as it should be.

Considering the basic necessities—the traditional trinity of food, clothing, and shelter—our society, American society, has met its responsibilities to the first two in better fashion than to housing. There is enough to eat in the aggregate. Our farm industry produces more than we as a nation can consume, although the distribution system could stand streamlining. At least Food Stamps assure that many people eat a minimum diet. And in my experience adequate clothing exists for every man, woman and child. Certainly, I have sorted enough surplus clothes at the Albuquerque Opportunity Center to last a lifetime. Make that two lifetimes.

Providing housing is where we have been remiss. We who compose the great American middle class live in comfortable houses with conveniences that would astound our ancestors. But too many others who share the stage with us in the current production of the human comedy remain "unhomed," the majority not by choice, believe me. To paraphrase the words of the boorish postal clerk: We have lots of work to do.

Now my musings turn to motivation, the why of it all. Why care about housing others? Despite life-long attempts to minimize navel-gazing, preferring at this very moment to set sail for a corny word play on naval-gazing, I cross-examine myself on the impetus for volunteering. We might as well ask why mountains are climbed, why bottle caps are collected, why images were painted in dank-and-dark caves by the ancients, or why a twenty-dollar bill was flipped into a stranger's vehicle by a putatively rational person. We as a race, the human race, often plunge into activities that defy practical explanations, volunteering among them.

I kiss off inquiries about why I volunteer by mouthing my familiar throw-away lines. "I need to do something to keep me occupied in retirement." Or, "I need to get out of the house and give my wife some peace and quiet." Or, "All play and no work makes Fred a dull boy."

More commonly, I parrot what I hear others say about "wanting to give something back." That's true enough, I guess, for someone who considers himself to have led a privileged life, if not a charmed life. Any objective accounting would post my name on the credit side of life's ledger.

Also, many like me were blessed with role models—parents in my case. In their class-bound way, my folks were community activists before the term gained popularity. From church, to school, to fraternal organizations, to politics, they were out and about in the community more than one night a week. As a child observing their activities, it's likely that I intended to honor that family tradition.

I cannot speak for others, but I am not motivated by fear or expectation of rewards, including the celestial variety. Let me give you a clue. I have not bothered to take harp lessons. Certainly, sainthood does not await me. Anyway, I believe a St. Frederick already exists, although when I jokingly mentioned this to an acquaintance, he reminded me that I could become "Saint Frederick of Albuquerque." Fat chance. Volunteering at the Albuquerque Opportunity Center or anywhere else will not gain me admittance to the Elysian Fields or any similar destination, any more than not volunteering will relegate me to a hotter location, although I've always preferred warm climates.

As for being a "do-gooder," I will wear that sticky tag if everyone acknowledges that in the best volunteer positions, we also are "get-gooders," deriving personal satisfaction from our experiences, often at a level topping our contributions. I would like to express this more creatively, but for the nonce a modified cliché will suffice: Perceived virtue is its own reward.

Then we must abide the cynics who, like the

poor, will always be with us. I get a whiff of condescension wafting downwind from those who proclaim—without proof—that volunteers are motivated by guilt. As reported in an earlier setting, I prefer to leave that one to Dr. Freud. But I hope that the good doctor would forgive the observation that if the pop-psyche prattle from these sideline observers bears any truth, we ought to salute guilt for all the good works it has spawned in recorded history. Rah, rah, guilt.

Whatever else is said about us, no one can relegate us into an armchair. We are not armchair liberals, or conservatives, or in between. No, we serve our causes on the battle's front lines where the rubber meets the road. (Don't you just love mixed metaphors?) By the way, as I drive along, the road analogy carries a personal touch, given the many miles racked up piloting the duty-hardened Gray Ghost around town.

Entertaining these jumbled thoughts does not trump my original sentiment that volunteering involves an act better felt than analyzed. Still, I cannot forgo one last navel gaze from the streets on a day that has spent its light.

Perhaps since the ancients organized themselves into tribes and began chilling out around campfires millennia ago, human beings have systematically, inexorably, and unconsciously adopted an inner sense of community. In olden days, community action may have derived more from the need to ensure the common defense than is the case nowadays. Regardless, individual action for community good seems to spring from something embedded within us that we cannot articulate, but rather something hard-wired into our beings as social animals. We seek to protect and preserve the community where we hold membership. The fuzzy—to me—terms "social maintenance" and "collective unconscious," perhaps gleaned from some long-ago graduate school classes, are craving to make nuisances of themselves, signaling that I have reached the point of fatigue with these mental gymnastics.

I appreciate that I am positing a half-baked hypothesis, and that I have staggered into the realms of sociology, psychology, anthropology, and even theology, not to mention other fields beyond my competence level—territory not unfamiliar to me.

Somewhere, sometime, I think I read that gilded members of the deep-think set—Charlie Darwin among them—have explored and expounded upon the subject of altruism, which may be the word and concept I have been fumbling for all along. I ought to bone up on that literature to help me sort things out in a more coherent fashion some day. But not today. My journey at an end, I have coasted into my floodlit driveway where domestic matters are barging their way into my uppermost thoughts. I'm home.

All royalties from *Our Sheltered Lives* will be donated to Albuquerque's Metropolitan Homelessness Project.

CPSIA information can be obtained at www.ICGtesting.com
Printed in the USA
LVOW08s1821290713

344944LV00009B/20/P